Toward a Contextual Realism

Toward a Contextual Realism

Jocelyn Benoist

Harvard University Press

CAMBRIDGE, MASSACHUSETTS . LONDON, ENGLAND

2021

Second printing

Library of Congress Cataloging-in-Publication Data

Names: Benoist, Jocelyn, 1968– author.
Title: Toward a contextual realism / Jocelyn Benoist.
Description: Cambridge, Massachusetts : Harvard University Press, 2021. |
Includes bibliographical references and index.
Identifiers: LCCN 2020042747 | ISBN 9780674248489 (cloth)
Subjects: LCSH: Realism. | Contextualism (Philosophy) | Intentionality
(Philosophy) | Ontology.
Classification: LCC B835 .B344 2021 | DDC 149/.2—dc23
LC record available at https://lccn.loc.gov/2020042747

Contents

Preface: Intentionality and Reality

TO WHAT KIND of worry should a statement of realism be a response? Probably, in the first place, a sense of having lost contact with the world.

The great accomplishment of the twentieth century was the discovery of the incredible richness and variety of the symbolic realm, of how many signs and codes articulate our relation to reality. Perhaps a downside of this huge step forward is the impression that all those signs and their codes merely separate us from reality by forming a kind of screen between it and ourselves. As though reality were concealed behind meaning and consequently—since meaning proves to be very complex—infinitely far from us.

Perhaps then realism should be understood as the affirmation that there *really is* something beyond the veil of meaning. What, however, should 'really' mean here? It is hard to make sense of what it could mean apart from signalling a kind of 'transcendence': there *really is* something that cannot be reduced to an idol of meaning, there is something that exists *beyond* meaning.

It is very tempting to translate this idea of the transcendence of reality to meaning into some kind of essential, metaphysical *meaninglessness*. As if reality needed to be meaningless in order to be truly beyond meaning.

This characterization, however, is equivocal. It can mean that reality is a category to which it makes no sense to apply the concept of meaning; reality *is just what it is*—that is its definition—and

vii

thus does not have meaning itself. However, on a substantial under-standing of 'meaninglessness,' it does not make sense to call reality 'meaningless.' For on that understanding, to call something 'mean-ingless' presupposes the possibility of its being 'meaningful,' in which case the notion of meaning applies to reality after all.

One powerful trend in contemporary philosophy has understood the meaninglessness of reality in the second sense, that is, *not as a categorical difference but as something more substantial*; as if meaninglessness were a positive property of reality.[1] Jean-Paul Sartre, for example, having avoided the pitfall of conceiving reality as an 'obstacle'—which is still a way of interpreting it from a per-spective which grants it some definite 'meaning'—insists on reali-ty's indifference to meaning, as though it were a kind of stupidity or, put differently, an essential, and apparently agonizing *meaningless-ness*. Reality, however, is not 'stupid': *it just is what it is*. Why should we feel a lack of meaning here? Is this not a way of once more mistakenly expecting something reality cannot give, not because of any kind of positive metaphysical impossibility, but simply be-cause it is a category mistake to think that reality could possess meaning?

It seems, however, that a large swathe of contemporary philos-ophy is convinced of having lost contact with reality to such an ex-tent that it feels the need to discover some kind of *break in meaning*, in order that it might recover the feeling of making contact with it again. An interesting example of this attitude can be found in the Italian philosopher Maurizio Ferraris's conversion to realism a few years ago, which he describes in his book *The External World*.[2] Fer-raris explains *cum grano salis* that he was, so to speak, *struck* by a reality beyond every construction or representation when he experi-enced an earthquake in his hotel room whilst staying in Mexico City. Of course, the anecdote speaks for itself precisely because that

1. One can find traces of this view at the core of 'speculative realism' as it has been framed by Meillassoux (2010).
2. Ferraris 2001.

particular instance of reality may well be beyond the reach of our familiar speech. The earthquake questions that very 'grounding soil' of evidence that Edmund Husserl highlighted as an essential basis for meaning. From that point of view, the image of the earthquake is powerful.

Now, it is necessary to ask how it comes to pass that a philosopher *needs anything like an earthquake in order to get real.* Reality is everywhere, not just in brutal breaks in or from meaning—not only in *what we cannot make sense of.* Why should reality necessarily take on the form of a catastrophe? This kind of view can correctly be described as a subtle form of negative anthropomorphism.

In fact, I do not think Ferraris himself endorses such a 'catastrophic view.' He believes, like everyone else, that the rooms we are all familiar with are just as real as an earthquake. What is interesting, however, is that he feels compelled to use that kind of example in order to make his point about the 'non-cancellability' *(inemendabilità)* of reality. Reality is, in some sense, 'stronger' than meaning—and at any rate independent of it. In this kind of argument we always find the same basic idea of reality's 'transcendence,' as if what primarily characterizes reality in its irreducibility is that it is *beyond* the sphere of meaning.

Now, from time to time making sense of reality presents a difficult challenge. That this is possible is surely an essential part of what we call 'reality.' It is an aspect of the concept of reality. But it would be a mistake to think that it forms the core of the concept—that it is, so to speak, reality's trademark.

This is firstly because, as we have mentioned, 'failing to correspond to human meaning' is a characterization of reality that remains *within* meaning and so, to some extent, makes the concept of reality dependent on meaning—at least in a negative way. Secondly, it seems important that when circumstances are favourable, meaning *is able to capture reality*—just as it is true that we can find *no meaning* for it when circumstances are unfavourable. Of course, the simple fact that we can succeed or fail in meaning something is already proof that meaning something occurs on solid ground. Both success and failure are only possible within reality.

Through this remark we have already switched from a point of view according to which reality is, or fails to be, *in front of* what we mean, to a point of view according to which it is, so to speak, *all around it*—its very *element*. I will return to this point at the end. However, let us first explore in greater depth the fact that if we succeed in meaning something, then—when what we mean is real—our meaning adequately captures the thing in its reality. Yet depending on the perspective we adopt, this assertion *may or may not turn out to be tautological*.

According to one perspective it *is* tautological, since—on a fairly central use of the word 'meaning'—nothing need be added to meaning in order for it to reach reality: this is just what meaning does. From a different perspective, saying that meaning—when successful—captures reality as such, is not to have said nothing. It is to insist on the fact that the 'the thing itself' is met within meaning. This presupposes that such a thing can be thought of as 'being itself.' Indeed, this is what we call its 'reality.'

Now, what does it mean to say 'the thing's being itself'? This is not an issue of identity. *For there is no identity without an identification.* The same thing can be identified in very different ways. This is an important aspect of meaning: our being able to identify what is meant *as* such and such. Now, for something to 'be itself' is just for it *to be the very thing it is*. 'Being itself' is not something that the thing can be *identified* as, except in very specific situations. This is what we can call the 'ipseity' or 'selfhood' of the thing. We can call *real* everything that has an ipseity, that is to say a being of its own. Or in other words, everything *real* is said to be in a sense of 'being' that is independent of being *meant*.

Now, in a lot of cases, meaning is concerned precisely with this ipseity—with 'things being themselves'—and it captures this *ipseity* wherever it succeeds. This is because the thing's being this or that is just a guise of its being itself. However, it would be a mistake to understand a thing's being what it is as a *borderline case* of its being this or that. In fact it would be a category mistake: 'being itself' is not—except in metaphysics—a way it makes sense to characterize something as being. Nevertheless, very often it is in view of the thing's 'being itself' that we say it is *this* or *that*. As such, *meaning concerns reality.*

We can say that what we mean *is real* whenever it *is* in an additional sense than that of simply being meant—although what is meant in this additional sense may well be the same as that which is meant. In other words, one of meaning's powers consists in being able to refer to the way things are in a sense other than the one found in the mere notion of *being meant*.

There is, therefore, no need to look for a realm *transcendent to meaning* in order to establish reality—as if reality were the sort of thing that *could* be established. It is enough to look at meaning: its claims and accomplishments. If we examine meaning we shall everywhere find reality as precisely that upon which meaning articulates a perspective. It makes no sense to say that reality as such is 'beyond' meaning: it is just what meaning, at least in many cases, is concerned with. Reality should not be confused with what meaning makes of it. That is just a category mistake. However, reality is not 'beyond' meaning either. *Sometimes* it is that for which we cannot find a meaning—we just do not know what to make of it—but *sometimes* it is exactly what is meant. Yet even in the latter case, reality is not simply identical to the meaning that captures it. Nor is it for that reason any less real than when we can find no meaning for it.

As a matter of fact, the false problem of reality's 'transcendent' nature results from the mistaken perspective according to which reality can be or fail to be *in front* of our meaning. On such a view, since it is not always clear whether meaning has a 'counterpart'— and because reality appears to play the role of such a counterpart—it is necessary sometimes for experienced reality to exceed whatever meaning we can find for it, as this excess is thought to provide *proof of the existence of the reality that lies in front of meaning.*

Now, the fact that, sometimes, we find ourselves lacking meaning for some things does not prove that there is any *intrinsic transcendence of those things to meaning* in general, but only that thus far we have not been able to find a meaning for them. This is a point about meaning rather than the things themselves. Conversely, the fact that sometimes we may actually doubt whether there really is anything 'in front' of meaning has to do with meaning as such: it just indicates that in those cases, we were not able to find a meaning that refers and thus in some sense any meaning at all (on a fairly central use of the word 'meaning' at least). It is not that, in front of meaning, there is something that is really lacking. The defect is in our meaning.

Thus, realism about meaning simply requires us to forswear this kind of 'frontal' perspective. What is much more at issue is our capacity to develop a perspective on reality—which is at least one dimension or usage of the concept of meaning. Now, this capacity is something that is only exercised within reality. Meaning is something that can neither refer to reality successfully—nor fail in doing so—'from outside.' Neither success nor failure are possible outside the realm of reality. Meaning itself, as a *mere* take on something, *is nothing real.* However, meaning as such—especially since in many cases it *concerns* reality—always presupposes reality as *its basis and the space of its conditions.* For we cannot mean anything without meaning it *from somewhere*—and, so long as we can standardize this somewhere and characterize those conditions, they always remain real. When analysing any particular meaning, one should always pay as much attention to its presuppositions regarding what is real—that is to say, the reality on which it rests and that makes it possible as the particular meaning it is—as to what it *claims* to be real. Reality is as much *upstream* from meaning as it is *downstream* of it.

That is a point about *context.* Once again: context is not so much an external constraint on meaning—as if reality, so to speak, struck meaning from the outside—as it is the manifestation of meaning being *effectively rooted* in reality, as well as something that contributes to the constitution of meaning itself. If meaning does not have to 'make contact' with reality, that is because it is already active as a genuine normative 'move' within the space of reality. In other words, meaning is a concrete way within a determinate situational framework (which can be more or less abstract), of having a take on some part of reality. One can mean something to be thus and so, only if, in the background, some things are what *they* are. Things being 'what they are' can in turn be characterized, *in other takings,* as being this or that. But it is important that in one take on reality, the background remains blind, remains mere 'reality.'

So, there is something decidedly misleading in a common way of formulating the realist position, as if the problem was how one can assert the presence of some sort of counterpart for our various meanings, one that might be missing. In fact the real task is to *situate* these meanings within reality whilst making sense of *the normative framework* they set up for this 'reality.' This way it is possible to see that, wherever meanings are effective, they *just are* contact with reality.

Once the *real conditions and purport* of meaning are understood, the epochal worry about the meaning's ability to make contact with reality turns out to be a worry about our meaning something much more than about whether or not things exist 'in front of' meaning. The problem should be reformulated this way: When are we *really meaning something?* Which is also to ask: When are we really *involved in our meaning, instead of remaining outside of it?* The doubt about our ability to mean anything *real* is, at bottom, a doubt about our capacity to mean anything at all. For it is an intrinsic question regarding meaning why one should ever be able to mean anything.

Chapter 1 was first published as "Why Should Inexistent Objects Be a Problem?" in *Intentionality. Historical and Systematic Perspectives,* edited by Alessandro Salice and published by Philosophia Verlag in 2012. Chapter 2 first appeared in print as "The Internal and the External in Knowledge," in *Rethinking Epistemology, vol.1*, edited by Günter Abel and James Conant Berlin and published by de Gruyter in 2012. Chapter 3 was published as "First Person is Not Just a Perspective: Thought, Reality and the Limits of Interpretation" in *Consciousness and Subjectivity*, edited by Sofia Miguens and Gerhard Preyer and published by Ontos Verlag in 2012. Chapter 9 appeared as "Making Ontology Sensitive," *Continental Philosophy Review*, vol. 45, no. 3, September 2012, p. 411–424. Chapter 10 was first published as "Realism Without Entities" in *Idealism, Relativism, and Realism*, edited by Dominik Finkelde and Paul Livingston and published by De Gruyter in 2020. The original texts appear here with minor edits.

I would like to thank Sandra Laugier, whose proximity made me who I am philosophically; James Conant, who taught me everything about philosophizing in the English-speaking world and who thus opened me up to a new way of practising philosophy, and Charles Travis, whose influence reshaped every problem for me, helping me out of so many pieces of philosophical nonsense. Thanks to Rory O'Connell, as well, who helped me revise my English text.

Toward a Contextual Realism

CHAPTER ONE

The Imaginary Subject of Intentional Objects

ACCORDING to one persistent philosophical tradition, the fact that what one takes to be the case might turn out not to be is problematic. How can I think *what is not*, given that, if I am thinking, there is therefore something that I think? On the other hand, *what* I am thinking might turn out not to be. As such, the thing in question appears both to be and not to be at the very same time.

This kind of worry gives rise to a whole host of problems concerning what have been dubbed 'intentional objects.' Intentional objects are objects of our mental attitudes. Their intentional being—that is, their being thought of—does not necessarily entail that they possess *genuine* being. Some hard-liners even claim that intentionality *excludes* genuine being, on the grounds that what exists intentionally never literally exists.

In his letter to Anton Marty of March 17, 1905, Franz Brentano makes the following grammatical point concerning the use of the term 'representation': "The representation *(Vorstellung)* does not include the 'represented thing,' but 'the thing,' as object; so, for instance, the representation of a horse does not include a 'represented horse,' but a 'horse' as object (immanently, that is to say describable exclusively as an *object* proper)."[1]

The representation is a representation of the thing itself. To say it is the representation *not* of the thing itself, but of 'the represented thing,' would merely make it *another representation*—very likely

---

1. Brentano 1930, p. 88. I give my own translation here, as the official one is not particularly accurate.

one that includes a further representation of *she who represents,* since the notion of a 'represented thing' is essentially relative to the one who is representing the thing in question. This grammatical point entails that there is a kind of *logical transparency* to what we call 'representation.' Being represented adds nothing to the thing. When something is represented, for example a horse, it is represented just as it is—nothing but the thing itself is represented. As such, the thing becomes an *object*—that is, the object of a representation.

'Object,' therefore, is a *functional* term. In his *Psychology from an Empirical Standpoint,* Brentano makes clear that he is perfectly aware of the scholastic use of the word 'object': 'object' means 'an object for the mind.' No object stands alone. The horse in the meadow is not in itself an object: it is a thing—an animate thing. This horse *functions*—wherever it is thought of—*as* an object of thought. The neglect of this scholastic distinction accounts for a sizeable number of the difficulties that have cropped up around the notion of intentionality in contemporary philosophy. An object might be a thing in its own right (e.g., the horse in the meadow). However, it is never necessary that such a thing, if real (a redundant qualification), is also an object.

Now, in the letter to Marty quoted above, Brentano goes on to say the following about the 'object': *"Dieses Objekt ist aber nicht."* At this point, the English translators recoil. They give: "But the object need not exist."[2] But this is not what is written. Saying this implies that, even if the object does not necessarily exist, it at least *might* have existed. However, this is not Brentano's point at all. He in fact writes: "But the object *is not.*" His meaning is perfectly clear: *the object as such—the object qua object—never exists.*

This assertion might sound paradoxical, as in the preceding analysis Brentano has not focused on the case of so-called fictional objects (e.g., centaurs), but has only used a horse as the example of a possible object of thought. Horses obviously exist; is it not possible

2. Brentano 1966, p. 77.

for me to think about the horse that is currently grazing in front of me in the meadow? Indeed, it would appear to be a very convenient object of representation if, as Brentano and a lot of philosophers after him held, a given perception is always based on a representation.

Brentano's point is that to exist as an object is not another, additional, kind of existence to that of the real thing (i.e., the thing that exists in the world). For to exist *as an object* is to not exist at all. In *Psychology From an Empirical Standpoint*, he warns us of the pitfalls surrounding the phrase 'to exist as an object.' He observes that the Scholastics "use the expression 'to exist as an object (objectively) in something,' which, if we wanted to use it at the present time, would be considered, on the contrary, as a designation of a real existence outside the mind."[3]

Modern linguistic usage (either in English or in German) has lost track of the scholastic sense of the term 'object.'[4] Consequently, when one says 'exist as an object,' one risks conceiving of it as a real 'existence,' despite the fact that being an object does not entail having any kind of existence. Strictly speaking, as far as an object is 'in the mind' it *is not.*

From the Scholastic point of view according to which the object is 'immanent'—and where this immanence is precisely what makes something an object—we can say that the object *is not.* But not in the sense that it does not *exist*—as if it *might* have existed—but in the sense that an 'object' is just not the kind of thing of which it is meaningful to say either that it does or does not exist. That sort of *ontological* determination is just not applicable to objects—to objects *as such*, that is. What exists or doesn't exist is the *thing* that happens to be an object of thought. Yet being an object of thought is not an additional ontological property of the thing. Nor is it some kind of *default being* that acts as a substitute wherever genuine being is lacking.

3. Brentano 1973, p. 88.
4. On Brentano's personal faithfulness to the scholastic sense of 'object,' see Courtine 2007, ch. II.

At this juncture, a new trend in Brentanian scholarship (cf. Antonelli,[5] Chrudzimski[6]) would emphasize the fact that there are different stages in the development of Brentano's thought. Indeed, Brentano did not always appear to be hostile to the idea of intentional beings. In his famous lecture, *On the concept of truth* (1889), he wrote that in the "correspondence *(Uebereinstimmung)* which holds between a true judgment and its object and the existence or non-existence of its object," there is nothing asserted concerning "a being in the sense of anything real, thing-like, entity-like *(Real, Dinglich, Wesenhaft).*"[7] Thus, he seemed decidedly open to the possibility of a kind of being that he would later rule out in the so-called 'reist' phase of his thought. A kind of being, that is, which we are told he had already ruled out in his earlier thought, that is, the being of an 'object' that is not a thing, nor anything that directly depends on a thing. In the quoted sentence, 'existence' and 'nonexistence' serve as properties of the object *(Gegenstand)* independently of whether or not it is a 'thing.' According to this terminology, 'to exist' is—as Husserl would later put it—just to be the object of a true judgment.

This 'intentional' conception of existence is certainly at odds with the 'reist' conception Brentano later developed. Nevertheless, the undeniable reality of this development should not tempt us to ascribe to him a full-blooded theory of 'intentional existence.' It is permissible to speak, around the time of the lecture *On the concept of truth*, of an 'intentionalist conception of existence' according to which something might be said to exist insofar as the mental act that posits it is justified. However, in this case, we are merely allowing that the object *exists*, where the being we ascribe to it is *being proper*—not merely 'intentional being.' Existence is *something with which we are dealing intentionally*, but it is not for all that an 'intentional existence.' Wherever the object is said to *exist*, it makes no sense to add that it exists 'intentionally'—as opposed to

5. Cf. Antonelli 2001.
6. Cf. Chrudzimski 2001.
7. Franz Brentano, "Ueber den Begriff der Wahrheit," § 54, in Brentano 1930, p. 25; Brentano 1966, p. 22 (amended translation).

what? It is not as if there were another existence besides existence! Of course, the things that can be said to exist are incredibly diverse. They come in many different varieties, some of which we might be reluctant to call 'things' at all—but that is a different problem.

One should acknowledge, therefore, that Brentano's ontology really did evolve (and was not continually 'reist'), without thereby losing track of the fact that he never accepted an ontology of intentional objects *as such*, according to which 'being in the mind' was a particular *kind* of being, one independent of the genuine existence of objects. Perhaps we should make room for a real diversity of genuine ways of being, some of which might turn out to be—for reasons found in reality itself—mind-dependent. However, we should never admit that being 'in the mind,' in the sense of intentional *inexistence*, is, by itself, a genuine way of being. In particular, within the framework of *On the concept of truth*, 'to be' is essentially a *polar* concept, and therefore only makes sense insofar as the opposition between being and nonbeing holds. If that is true, how can we make sense of an unconditional 'intentional being' of what is 'in the mind'? On the contrary, the relevant question is: Does the so-called object we have 'in our mind' exist or not?

Thus, according to Brentano—the philosopher who renewed the concept of intentionality at the dawn of contemporary philosophy—*there is no room for an ontology of intentional objects;* that is to say, objects 'in the mind' in the intentional sense of the term. This topic is essentially imaginary,[8] for one of the most entrenched principles of Brentano's philosophy is that *to be represented* is not—in any sense—*to be.* Introducing anything like an *esse diminutum* simply amounts to a category mistake, one that distorts the border between what is and is not ontology.

Why is it then that the temptation of an 'intentional ontology' an ontology of intentional objects constituting their own ontological

---

8. In a sense of 'imaginary' identical to Peter Strawson's when he writes about the 'imaginary subject of transcendental psychology' (Strawson 1966, p. 32) in Kant.

domain—has proven remarkably resilient within contemporary intentionalism[9] despite the explicit reluctance of the tradition's
founding father? Probably because, to rephrase Plato's *Sophist*
slightly, it is natural to assume that when one thinks, there must be
something one thinks about. Yet sometimes it is the case that the
'something' one is thinking about cannot be said <u>to be</u> in the sense
of actually existing—at least not in *true negative existential judgments*. Thus, the temptation arises to grant some 'quasi-ontological'
status to the thing the thought seems to be about and which nevertheless does not exist. It is as though there were *a way for things to
be, despite them not existing.*

The philosophical question we must address is as follows: What conception of thought and of thought's referentiality results in such a
predicament? At the root of the problem is the obvious fact that
what we think might not be the case. This is part of what *defines*
thought: to think, is to take something *to be* or *to be thus-and-so*;
yet sometimes what we take to be, or take to be thus-and-so, does
not exist or is not such-and-such. If that is true, what is the status of
what is thought when what is thought is not the case? Does the corresponding true thought not require the *existence* of what is thought
in order for it be a thought at all? This is the problem of so-called
'intentional entities.'

Now, this problem seems to stem from a mistaken conception of
the constitutively referential character of thought, specifically its
normativity. There are in fact two ways to interpret Plato's claim
that *thought must be about something*. As is well-known, in *The
Sophist* Plato seems to consider the possibility of distinguishing the
something *(ti)* from the being *(on)*, only to reject it:[10] "It is plain that

9. That is, the philosophical tradition that takes intentionality to be the fundamental concept in the philosophy of mind.

10. On the possibility of 'tinology' (the science of the *ti* as such) and Plato's dis-
carding it in favour of 'ontology,' the science of *on*, see Aubenque 1991 and Courtine
1990, pp. 535–536.

in speaking of something we speak of being, for to speak of an abstract something naked and isolated from all being is impossible."[11]

Thus, when Plato observes that thinking—and therefore speaking since, in his view, thought is nothing but *the soul's conversation with itself*—is necessarily *thinking about something*, he surely means thinking about some *being*. Although he finally makes room for the possibility of a thought that does not think of things as they really are—a *false* thought—it remains the case in his view that thinking is thinking about *something that is*. There is a basic priority of being to thought, which is exactly what we encounter in the idea of thought having an essentially referential character: there is no thought without there being, in the first place, a being to think of. The solution to the problem of the False that Plato finally devises does not jettison this basic ontological commitment on thought's part but on the contrary presupposes it. Thought remains true to this commitment even where what we think about the thing thought of is incorrect.

In order to make full sense of this we should do as Plato does at the end of the dialogue: pay proper attention to the grammar of what it is 'to think.' Ordinarily, to think is *to think something about something*. What we think is true or false. But such thoughts are of something. As such, there is *something about which* we think what we do. Now, Plato's point is that this 'something' must *exist*. A thought is necessarily about something that *exists*, even if it is mistaken regarding it. This insight—that even falsity entails a *presupposition*—is a magnificent one, and something we must retain. We can say there is no *absolute* falsity, insofar as what is false is 'false *of*' something, and can be such insofar as some contact has been made with the thing of which it is false.

Now, if this were merely a formal point about predication—as it perhaps appears to be in the final part of *The Sophist*—it would in fact be genuinely suspect. Is it not obvious that we sometimes

---

11. Plato, *The Sophist*, 237d, in Plato 1953, vol. III, p. 387.

predicate something of something that does not exist, as for instance when we say that Chiron was the teacher of Achilles, or in other examples so dear to friends of intentional objects?

One possible response to this objection is that such uses are localized—for example, within the contexts of fiction or assumptions in mathematics—and so very likely parasitic in some way on the standard, 'realist' mode of predication. To predicate something of something is in the first place to determine how things *are*, which presupposes *that* they are. Derivatively—but only derivatively—this might give rise to forms of pseudo-predication that are not themselves ontologically committed but that parody ontological predications, so to speak.

Obviously this does not constitute a proof, only a *petitio principii*. The real question is what induces us to think that thought essentially concerns reality (ignoring, that is, the cases above that don't threaten this idea)?

To this question, there is no other response than to observe the ordinary way in which we use the verb 'to think.' To think, ordinarily, is to adopt some stance toward the world. This is the *primary* use of the verb 'to think.' The way we think directly bears upon how we see the world—the way we take the world to be. 'Would you say he is my age?' is a question about how the world is, just as 'Don't you think he will come?' is a question about how the world will be. In neither case are we asking about anything that lacks being or is independent of the world. This is what thinking is usually concerned with; it is highly likely that, were it not, we would understand by the word 'thought' something substantially different than we in fact do. What is at stake here is the basic world-relatedness (and therefore being-relatedness) of thought. To repeat, this relatedness is *normative*, which essentially means that thought, in the full-blooded sense of the term, is answerable to the world.[12] It is precisely how we *take things to be*. This is the primary sense of 'thought.'

12. On the notion of answerability, see Travis 2006, e.g., pp. 177–178.

Now, this does not exclude there being other, less ontologically committed ways of thinking (and, correspondingly, meanings of 'thinking'), but they will be derivative and in some sense secondary. The proof of this is that they make sense only against the backdrop of the basic relatedness of thought to being. What else is fiction, for instance, but the *alteration* of our basic commitment to the world as it is? The significance of fiction presupposes not our ignorance of reality, but rather the primacy of our sensitivity *to* reality.

So, even if from a formal perspective thought is not always about a particular being, its constitutive *aboutness* always presupposes some kind of relation to being that has already been established. This relation to being is, so to speak, the *basis* of thought. This might be a (liberal) way of understanding the Platonic requirement. On this reading, the requirement comes down to an acknowledgment of the basic worldliness of thought and a simultaneous acceptance of the fact that thoughts allow of different degrees of commitment to the world—not just *any* thought claims to capture a real state of affairs.

From this perspective, even if in order to make sense of some particular mental attitudes we have to grant referential status to non-existing entities (e.g., a fictional character such as Madame Bovary), it would be utterly mistaken to *generalize* from this and think that thought *in general* refers to such entities. What we might call *the referentiality of thought* is in the fundamental case (that which plays the role of a standard for the deviant / secondary cases) thought's relatedness to some part of the world which it concerns, and of which it is either true or false. To adopt a vocabulary loosely connected to Barwise and Perry's: in the fundamental case *a thought is about a situation*, concerning which it is true or false; this situation is in some sense the 'referent' of the thought. The worldly rootedness of thoughts through which they pick something out as their object, is, in the primary case, something essential to them. Their object, then, is not something intentional, but a real thing or, as we might say, a real 'situation.'

An alternative way of dealing with this issue is to only allow for reference at the level of *terms*. The idea, loosely Wittgensteinian, is that the objects corresponding to terms *necessarily exist*, whereas the combination of objects that the picture as a whole presents *do not necessarily exist*. If we allow the traditional assimilation of 'representations' and mental terms, this alternative holds that the objects of representation always exist, but that they are not necessarily always combined in the way our thought takes them to be.

This alternative might provoke resistance analogous to that elicited by our earlier observation regarding the constitutive aboutness of thought, for it is clear that sometimes we represent *things that do not exist*. However, on one philosophical notion of representation, according to which representation is *below the level of explicit ontological claims* (this notion can be found in the traditional contrast between *representation* and *judgment*) the point is not so much that what is represented *exists*, but that it is always already *taken to exist*. As such, what is represented is not something whose existence is in question; it merely underpins questions of existence, so to speak. From this point of view, what is represented by the terms featuring in a complete thought—the objects—is broadly identified with whatever is *taken for granted*. Of course, this analysis still rests on the conception of thought we advanced above, according to which a complete thought bears a commitment to the world.

However, another notion of 'representation' is conceivable. Perhaps representation does not designate a sublevel of what is thought (in the full-blooded sense of 'thought'), but instead designates *what is thought* in a way which brings with it a kind of *ontological indifference*. On this understanding of representation I might represent something while knowing perfectly well that there is no such thing, and so the representation does not entail even a tacit recognition on my part of something's existing. This is more or less what is expressed in English by the phrase *'to think of.'* Looking at the hearth whilst digesting my Christmas dinner, I think of a salamander. Obviously I do not thereby commit myself to the existence of such a creature. My 'free' (i.e., ontologically noncommittal) representation does not require that I so commit myself. This is another sense of the word 'representation.'

Now, as in the previous analysis, the mistake is to take these senses to be identical, reading the latter into the former. Is every thought, in the 'full-blooded' sense of the term, made up of representations? It is obvious that in one merely logical sense they are. Representations are simply *what thoughts are made out of:* they are the basis of thoughts. However, what is primary here is *the thought itself:* the representations depend on the thought in virtue of being its functional parts, and thus they possess sense only in the context of the thought.

However, in another way it is not at all obvious, for a full-blooded thought does not require that anything be represented in that dreamy, non-committed sense of 'representation.' Real thoughts are not made of dreams. One might even say that they exclude them, at least to some extent. Of course, one might prefer to say that this sense of 'representation' opens the possibility of there being yet *another sense of 'thought.'* Once again, the question comes down to what one means by 'thought' and the possible diverse meanings the word may possess.

Representationalism is the view that there is a *basic* ontologically non-committal sense of 'thought,' and that it is only on the basis of thoughts understood in this sense that it is possible to construct committed thoughts. *Anti-Representationalism*, the position that amounts to the rejection of this idea, is not ignorant of the fact that the word 'thinking' has diverse meanings and that on some of them thinking is not ontologically committed. The real question is one of priority. Are there senses of 'thought' that involve no commitment, neither secondary nor basic? That is the question.

Getting back to our problem concerning intentional objects, we can now say that whether we grant them ontological or non-ontological status depends on what global conception of thought and its relation to the world we endorse.

As a matter of fact, what makes possible the problem of the ontological status of intentional objects is a conception according to which thought is in principle cut off from the world. It is as if thought were a realm in itself, a 'kingdom within a kingdom' and the real question were whether it connected or failed to connect with the world from 'outside.' In that case, it is possible to conceive *the object of thought* as something existing by itself, dependent merely on the act of thought or an attitude, despite the fact that the very same act or attitude is answerable to the world. Again, this might be the case with certain states of mind that could be considered 'thoughts' (and why shouldn't they be?). However, the only question is whether we are willing to consider this situation a standard example of what we call 'thought.'

This problem of thought's connection to the world—as well as its offspring, the problem of so-called 'intentional objects' that function as *general* features of our thought (not confined, that is, to particular contexts)—is typical of modern epistemology.

Now the other perspective, which is perhaps more traditional, emphasizes the essential world-relatedness of thought. From this perspective it appears likely that the problem of thought's connection to the world is a pseudo-problem that results from the fact that the basic connection between thought and world has been severed by a poor epistemology, one that relies on an inadequate analysis of *thought*. It is as if thought could float free of the world. Yet what could such thoughts be? Modern epistemology frequently treats thoughts in isolation, both from the world and one another. But it is very difficult to see how one can make sense of them—in particular their *identity*—in this way.

As such, the time has come to ask whether it would not be better return to a conception of thought more in line with ancient philosophy, a conception on which thought's ontological commitment is the fully disclosed starting point. That would bring an end to a lot of preposterous questions about intentional objects and their so-called 'being.' There is no being except *genuine* being—there is no room for *'merely intentional being.'* Of course, this does not mean that such questions cannot take on meaning in *local contexts*. But they must be discarded *as general questions* regarding the essence of thought 'überhaupt.'

This means that, normally at least, being 'intended' is not a particular status something can bear, but rather something that happens to it, something which presupposes its existence and is grounded in its being. As such, thought is essentially related to the world, but *the intentionality of thought is not a two-way relation.* Aristotle makes this perfectly clear in a passage to which the friends of intentionality in contemporary philosophy should have paid more attention, and that probably underlies a very important observation of Brentano's in the first appendix to *Psychology from an Empirical Standpoint.*

Brentano writes that "where Aristotle enumerates the various main classes of his category of πρός τι (relation) he mentions mental reference," but adds that he "does not hesitate to call attention to something which differentiates this class from the others. In other relations both terms—both the fundament and the terminus—are real, but here only the first term—the fundament—is real."[13] Brentano infers from this that intentionality *is not a real relation*, and that the intentional object must be called 'relative-like' *(Relativliches)* rather than relative *(Relatives)* in the proper sense, since, if intentionality is a relation, it is a relation without terminus.

However, one might make the point from the reverse direction and say that, when our thought is about something that really *is*, it is still incorrect to describe the thing in question as 'relative,' as the relation of intentionality is *extrinsic to it*. Our thought in this case— which, *pace* modern internalism, is the *normal case*—is relative to

13. Brentano 1973, p. 271.

the (real) thing, but the thing, as such, is in no way relative to our thought.

This is what Aristotle says in a wonderful passage of *Metaphysics*, Δ, 15. A thought is relative to something, which is, in the basic case, a thing (or some feature of a thing). But to describe something as 'what that thought is relative to' would be to say nothing at all. "The thought is not relative to 'that of which it is the thought,' writes the Philosopher, for we should then have said the same thing twice."[14] What determines and identifies the thought is *what the thought is about*—that is, how things are with the thing—and precisely not this thing *only as the object of a thought:* the latter is circular and leads nowhere. This circularity is identical to the one that we saw was widespread in the misguided philosophical discourse surrounding 'intentional objects.'

14. Aristotle, *Metaphysics*, Δ, 15, 1021a30-32, translated into English by David Ross, in Aristotle 1984, vol. II, p. 1612.

CHAPTER TWO

Internalism and Externalism in Knowledge

EXTERNALISM is one of the core topics of contemporary epistemological debate. It might seem obvious that the concept of knowledge necessitates some form of *externality*. What is knowledge, after all, but a relation to things as they are in themselves? The concept of knowledge seems to presuppose that things are what they are independently of any alleged knowledge of them.

Of course, there are complicated cases in which it is difficult to maintain that such independence obtains. Some things are what they are *because* they are known. Furthermore, there is the question of what should be said about cases in which one's own knowledge is the very thing known. One cannot dismiss such cases—those of reflexive knowledge—and indeed, it is far from obvious that such reflexivity should not be considered *absolute,* on pain of embarking on an infinite regress.

None of this diminishes the fact that fundamental to the concept of knowledge is the idea of 'things as they are in themselves' that are a nonnegotiable in any given act of knowing. Sometimes it turns out that the things known are the way they are as a result of their being known. But, provided the act of knowledge is in place, the things known are simply thus and so and their being such exhibits an absolute norm for knowledge: one of *logical exteriority* to which knowledge is represented as essentially having to conform.

Now, if what is known essentially has just that kind of *logical independence* from knowledge, it may turn out that sometimes the independence is not only logical, but also factual. In fact, this is quite common. It occurs in all those cases that are traditionally described as 'knowledge of the external world.' This label is deeply equivocal and rests on dubious ontological assumptions, including the presumed distinction between 'interiority' and 'exteriority' as two separate kinds of ontological domain. Nevertheless, independently of these assumptions, which I am not going to discuss here, it is possible to give a *minimal, merely logical sense to such a division.* For instance, we can define 'knowledge of the external world' as precisely that which is characterized by the *factual* independence of knowledge's object from such knowledge.

Instances of what we might call 'external knowledge' are fairly common. It is even possible to say that they constitute the fundamental kind of knowledge from which the general sense of the word 'knowledge' is largely derived. It is highly probable that there is a phenomenological priority to *factual* independence, one that informs our capacity to make sense of the *logical* independence that belongs to the object of knowledge as such.

Now, wherever there is factual independence, something, or even many things, is liable to change. Or, in other words, what is known can change independently of my knowledge of it. It is necessary to assess the consequences of such changes for knowledge. Herein lies the problem of *epistemic externalism:* the constitutive exposure of knowledge to the factual externality of its object, that is, to something that knowledge itself cannot entirely control. This exposure appears to follow inevitably from the objectively external commitment of knowledge understood as knowledge of 'things as they are in themselves.' Let us explore in greater depth the nature of this 'externality.'

If knowledge, or at least some basic kind of knowledge, is essentially knowledge of something that *is* independently of such knowledge, it seems that we must distinguish between the thing's being known and the thing's being *simpliciter.* It is clear that if something is external to one's knowledge of it, it may have many facets that are *not* contained in one's knowledge:

"There are more things in heaven and earth, Horatio,
Than are dreamt of in your philosophy."[1]

Furthermore, there is no knowledge that does not occupy a particular *perspective*. What is of interest regarding a cow is not the same for the farmer, the artist, and the butcher. What it is to know a cow—as a cow—is therefore not the same for each of them. This does not mean that, from the perspective of one of them, that which constitutes the others' perspectives is not knowledge—but it is not what she immediately includes in her own notion of what is to know a cow. Every part of reality allows for an infinite variety of perspectives, and, in this sense, it lies beyond the perspective of any particular piece of knowledge that takes it as an object. This limitation is not a flaw in knowledge: it is simply its definition. Knowledge, as such, is perspectival—is 'knowledge *from a certain point of view . . .*'

Now, the fact that not everything concerning the object is known, and that one particular knowledgeable perspective leaves room for others, does not entail that a particular instance of knowledge *fails* to be knowledge. This intrinsic limitation of knowledge is not the negation of knowledge as such.

To know the front of a building is not to know the back of it, and, in some sense, nor is it to know the whole building—at least not with the comprehensiveness that might be required in some contexts. There are always an infinite number of things one could know about something, and so, in absolute terms, there always remains something more to know about it. On the other hand, to know the pig in the way a farmer does is not to know it in the same way that a naturalist does. So when my friend Denis, who is a fervent naturalist, insists on the fact that *only* the biologist can really know the pig because he is the one capable of analysing its DNA, it is difficult to make sense of what he is saying, for it is clear that, in another sense, the farmer *knows* it. The whole question turns on what kind of knowledge is considered relevant in a particular context. This problem of relevance is a core issue

1. William Shakespeare, *The Tragedy of Hamlet*, I, 5, 167–8, in Shakespeare 1899, p. 52.

of every epistemology. In other words: there is always an infinite number of senses in which something can be said to be known.

At any rate, knowing the front of a building from a cognitive perspective—that is, as a possible object of knowledge—is already knowing something; the fact that there are certainly other things to know about the building does not undermine its status as knowledge. On the other hand, knowing a pig from the perspective particular to the farmer is not to know it from the perspective of the naturalist, and in certain contexts the farmer's knowledge might prove more or less valuable than the naturalist's. But it is certainly knowledge—despite the fact that what it means to *know* the very same thing could, as a matter fact, turn out to be one of many different things.

Thus, the logical externality of some basic kinds of objects requires, firstly, some modesty on our part: there is always something additional to be known in the object beyond *our* knowledge of it. Secondly, it requires some capacity of adjustment (accommodation) on our part, since there is always a diversity of cognitive perspectives that are available, from which we must find one relevant to this particular context. However this two-sided externality is no objection to the idea that it is possible to have knowledge of the object. The fact that all our knowledge is limited both in its scope and its relevance does not make it void; it is simply part of what knowledge is.

However, it is tempting to say that, by virtue of being partial, all knowledge—or at least what appeared to be knowledge—is liable to be invalidated after the fact. For what I learn about something after further investigation can end up conflicting with what I thought I already knew about it. This will lead me to retrospectively discard what I at first took to be genuine knowledge. Whenever I assert that I know something, it seems this possibility can never be entirely excluded. For how can I distinguish *knowing* from *believing I know* on a merely *internal* basis? It appears the externality of the object is capable of rendering the status of the mental state that refers to it uncertain. Is it knowledge? On the basis of the evidence I have, I might be firmly convinced it is, although, in fact, it is not: some additional evidence would belie this conviction.

In a classic paper Norman Malcolm makes a distinction that is relevant to this issue. He claims that we should distinguish two different senses of 'know':

> When I use 'know' in the weak sense I am prepared to let an investigation (demonstration, calculation) determine whether the something that I claim to know is true or false. When I use 'know' in the strong sense I am not prepared to look upon anything as an investigation; I do not concede that anything whatsoever could prove me mistaken; I do not regard the matter as open to any question; do not admit that my proposition could turn out to be false, that any future investigation could refute it or cast doubt on it.[2]

If this distinction is not merely psychological, then it is a deeply peculiar one. No doubt our degree of certainty regarding what we take ourselves to know on particular occasions comes in varying degrees. Sometimes when someone says 'I know,' they will forswear this 'knowledge' if even gently pressed. But should we distinguish two kinds of knowledge, or two meanings of the verb 'to know,' just because of this? It is unclear that we should, for to say 'I know' involves a kind of *commitment*. It necessarily involves taking *a cognitive risk*—a risk that is not taken, for instance, in saying 'I believe.' Although it is true that whenever one says 'I believe' there is some kind of cognitive claim being made, the question as to its truth remains to some extent open, and so the risk taken when claiming to have knowledge is absent: a belief can turn out to be *mere belief*—and therefore not knowledge—whilst still remaining a belief.

As John Langshaw Austin observed in this context, 'I believe' is a descriptive expression. But apart from the presence in me of a particular mental state, it commits itself to nothing.[3] This is precisely not the case with the canonical use of the verb 'to know': when I say

2. Malcolm 1952, p. 183.
3. Austin 1961, p. 78.

'I know,' I am not just describing the state in which I find myself, but genuinely making a claim about *how things are*. The fact that I might be mistaken does not diminish my commitment in the slightest—it does not admit of degrees. I can believe something to lesser or greater degree. In a different sense, I can know something to a lesser or greater degree (e.g., a particular field). But I cannot say of some knowledge that I do have that it is knowledge "to some degree." I either claim to know it or not to know it. If I am not sure, and I'm being honest, I refrain from saying 'I know.' Instead I say: 'I believe.'

Does this mean that when I say 'I know' what I thereby take to be a genuine instance of knowledge can never be called into question? Certainly not: for this is often the case where what I claim to know is an *external object* in the logical sense we have introduced. The point, however, is that in saying 'I know' I attempt to shield what I say from such doubts—I claim it to be true *no matter what*. When I say that I know that there is a house before me, it is true that it might be a mere *façade* such as are found on movie sets. But in saying that I know that there is a house before me this possibility has been objectively excluded, regardless of whether or not I have ever actually entertained it.

Now, the fact that I may not have every reason that I could have for believing what I do does not entail that my claim is anything less than a knowledge claim. Moreover, it does not entail that my knowledge is anything less than a genuine instance of knowledge. The whole point is: What does 'every reason' mean here?

In the previous example it seems that I cannot be certain that there really is a house before me until I have checked the other side of it. Similarly, my friend Denis, an inveterate naturalist, can, upon seeing a chess player protect her king, wonder whether she really is protecting her king or simply moving at random—or even whether she is a chess player or a real human being at all. However, it seems that if we have *no particular reason* to think that these are mere 'façades' then we take ourselves to be seeing houses when we see 'façades'—or in other words, we take ourselves to be seeing 'façades *of* houses.' And, if we have *no particular reason* to think otherwise, we take ourselves to be seeing a chess player protecting her king when the person before us, in a particular context, makes a move in what we understand to be a game of chess.

In any given instance of 'external knowledge' it could so happen that a condition on its being knowledge—one that has hitherto remained unquestioned—has not in fact been met, such that the alleged knowledge turns out not to be knowledge at all, but merely belief. In which case we *believe*, but wrongly so—in spite of all the good reasons for belief to which we may be privy.

However, this is not what we mean when we say we *know* something, even if we're mistaken about knowing it. We do not say that we *believe*, but something further—something different. We mean that, whatever else might be the case, what we say is not false. We affirm that the conditions on our having knowledge are met, *whatever they may be.* Of course, since we cannot know all of these conditions— there is no exhaustive list of them, only an *open* list—we therefore take some kind of risk: a cognitive one. What looks like an instance of knowledge may eventually turn out to be a mere *belief.* Nevertheless, this possibility should not lead us to equate the concepts of knowledge and belief. To claim that one knows something is just to rule out all the hitherto open possibilities that what one believes might turn out not be the case—possibilities that nevertheless appear to be an intrinsic part of the very idea of *belief.* A belief can be both true and held with some conviction. However, to treat it as a belief means leaving open the theoretical possibility that it is false—even when *subjectively* no such possibility can be imagined. When one says '*I know,*' this theoretical possibility is discarded.

Now the mere rejection of this possibility is not sufficient in itself for attributing knowledge to someone. It seems that in order for me to be able to claim knowledge of something, it is necessary that the exclusion of this possibility (of there being any invalidating conditions) is *justified*, at least as far as I know. For example, if I am visiting a movie set for a Western and have been shown a whole array of façades without real houses behind them, then I cannot say I know there is a house in front of me when I see a façade on set—not in the full-blooded sense that the word 'house' has in everyday life. In this context I cannot know there is a house before me on the basis of what I see. I must examine further (i.e., take a look at the other side) in order to know for sure. Conversely, it seems that in everyday contexts I can, on the very same perceptual basis, say that I know there is a house across the street.

The fact that I can say 'I know' with authority does not necessarily mean that I am *right* in saying it. Indeed, unbeknownst to me there may have been demolition works on this block and a mere façade could be standing between two real buildings. However, that is very unlikely. As such it *makes sense* for me to say 'I know that these façades are the fronts of real houses,' even if this assertion might ultimately prove false—and so not expressive of knowledge, but of a mistake on my part.

On the other hand, it does not make sense for me to say 'I know' if there is an *obvious* possibility in a particular context that I have neglected to consider. In that case it is logical for someone to ask: 'Do you *really* know?' As long as I have failed to examine what the situation calls for me to examine, it is not appropriate for me to say 'yes.' The point therefore is that although the notion of *true* belief brings with it the required transcendence in virtue of being true, this does not by itself render it knowledge. One might have a true belief that is *not sufficiently justified in context,* so that it is in fact incorrect to call it knowledge—while for all that it is nonetheless *true.*

The very idea of knowledge involves the notion of justification. *We only know something if we have reasons for thinking it, at least to the extent that such reasons are required in context.* This is the basis of the old Aristotelian dictum that to know the truth by accident is not to know the truth at all. As such, knowledge is never a mere encounter with an exteriority. It presupposes that one has made that exteriority one's own, that one has internalized it as part of one's knowledge, as something that *one has reasons for taking to be the case.*

Nevertheless, it remains true that whenever knowledge is 'external knowledge' in the sense we have introduced, it is never the case that justification, however strong it might be, is enough to turn a belief into an instance of knowledge. We might be perfectly justified in context for *thinking* something that turns out to be false. This is the source of the literature that has flourished in contemporary epistemology under the name of 'Gettierology.'[4]

To see the relevance of the problem to our considerations, let us elaborate on Julien Dutant and Pascal Engel's liberal adaptation of Edmund L. Gettier's argument.[5] Let us suppose that, on the funicular that ascends the Vomero, a clever Neapolitan pickpocket has relieved me of my wallet. Upon seeing there is nothing valuable in it and fearing the consequences of my noticing the loss, he puts the wallet back in my pocket without my knowing. Do I know, at this point, that I have my wallet in my pocket? I have no reason to believe it is gone. I even have 'every reason' to think it is there, for I put it there, and we do not live in a world in which objects simply vanish. Thus, I rely on the presence of my wallet, and I feel perfectly authorized to say I know where it is—knowledge that would be confirmed by my double-checking, since the wallet is definitely where I believe it to be.

So, it might be the case that, although we have every reason—*as far as reasons are called for here*—to take things to be as they in fact are, we are still in some way misled: our reasons themselves might be misleading. After all, the pickpocket might have kept the wallet. The fact that he put it back and that everything is as if nothing had ever happened does not mean that nothing in fact happened, or that the wallet is where it is for the precise reasons I take it to be there.

---

4. See Gettier 1963.
5. Dutant and Engel 2005, pp. 13–14.

Of course, everything in this story is contextual. If, for instance, we are participating in a game where the objective is to take the other players' wallets by stealth as many times as possible, each of us could never be absolutely sure of having our wallet, and it is questionable whether we would ever be able to say we *know* we have our wallet. And if David Avadon calls me up to the stage, how can I claim to *know* that I have my wallet?

In fact, it is not so difficult to imagine such cases transpiring in everyday life: let us suppose that in some part of the city pickpocketing has become endemic and that the pickpockets are so careful and so dextrous (always replacing the owner's wallet after helping themselves) that they generally go unnoticed. In this case, what does it mean *to know* that one has one's wallet? In such conditions, you are certainly not wrong to claim that you have your wallet: you have it—though not in the way that you thought you did, for the wallet might have been emptied of its contents. However, if someone says they *know* they have their wallet they are not quite right—for they do not have their wallet *in the way they took themselves to have it.*

This result sounds paradoxical, for it seems reasonable to think the following regarding the *transparency* of knowledge: if I am right in thinking that *p*, do I not *know* that p? Sometimes it is tempting to say: 'she knows that p, though not for the right reasons.' After all, in some contexts this may not be so absurd. Sometimes what matters is simply the fact that *she knows that p*, regardless of whether her reasons are good ones. Thus, it is not impossible to talk, in certain circumstances, of 'knowledge by mistake'—or on the 'basis of a mistake.' Everything depends on whether the emphasis is placed on *the mere grasp of a particular fact*, or on *the way this grasp is obtained.* What does or does not count as knowledge is not always clear.

However, this relative standard of what counts as knowledge is not something *generalizable:* in a particular circumstance it is normally very clear whether a claim amounts to knowledge or not, even when our reasons for thinking what we do are not quite adequate in particular circumstances. On the one hand, it depends on the content of the alleged knowledge, and, on the other hand, how peculiar the circumstances are relative to the background against which the kind of knowledge claims in question are usually made. Of course, as with everything peculiar or abnormal, the challenge to our usual standards of what our knowledge amounts to cannot always be anticipated: 'hard cases' can arise. However, they are the *logical* exception—*otherwise the very idea of knowledge would make no sense.*

If what we have called 'external knowledge'—that is, knowledge of things *as they are*—is genuine knowledge (and it must be, for it largely determines the sense of 'knowledge' more generally), then it puts us in touch with the externality of things. It is thus exposed to the vicissitudes of this externality, to such an extent that we might even wind up being deceived in thinking that a true belief is an instance of knowledge. For it can happen that the very basis of our knowledge is undermined without our noticing and without what we take ourselves *to know* being rendered false.

However, it would be incorrect to draw the conclusion that, since no external knowledge is absolutely immune to the possibility of 'cancellation' and subsequent reclassification as 'true belief,' that therefore there is no such thing as external knowledge. Something can be cancelled only against a background in which the idea of its existence makes sense in the first place. We must guard against a perverse generalization of the argument.

Imagine that objects in the world only existed intermittently, but on such an infinitesimally small temporal scale that we were never phenomenologically aware of their discontinuity. Perhaps this supposition sounds weird. But doesn't our problem concern possibilities that we can never absolutely exclude, such as the possible 'weirdness' of nature? After all, who *knows* what might turn out to be the case? That said, we can still ask: is the hypothesis really an objection to the notion that we have knowledge of objects that endure in time?

In the sense of endurance that microphysicists are interested in, it certainly is. But then the question is: Is this the kind of endurance at issue in our ordinary knowledge of enduring objects? It seems not: even if the existence of the object suffers from supposed 'micro-breaks' below the threshold of our perception, what counts is the macroscopic continuity of the object we perceive, touch, and generally have dealings with. This is what we normally mean by 'endurance.' If these conditions of 'endurance' are satisfied, then we certainly have knowledge of enduring objects.

However, if I've substituted my daughter's goldfish for another without her knowing, she cannot be said to know she has the same goldfish, not in the sense *she* takes herself to have the same goldfish—for it is not the same fish. And if, afterward, I put the first fish back into the tank, swapping it for the substitute goldfish, she still cannot be said to know that she has the same fish—even if it is true that she does, and even if she is justified in believing this (for she has no reason to suspect I am engaging in such peculiar behaviour).

Every instance of knowledge thus has *real limits:* it is always the case that special circumstances can disqualify its status as knowledge. However, these limits belong to the same level, so to speak, as the knowledge in question does. The special circumstances that can create a justificatory gap have to be such that they affect the relevant justification. Whatever happens 'below' that level is irrelevant for these purposes. Of course, it is not always so easy to distinguish these levels, and that is just part of what we have called 'externality.'

Now, the possibility of there being factual limits at the very level at which a knowledge claim resides—a possibility that always remains open—does not mean that we should supplement every knowledge claim with some qualification in the manner Austin describes in an ironical passage of 'Other Minds':

> If you are aware you may be mistaken, you oughtn't to say you know, just as, if you are aware you may break your word, you have no business to promise. But of course, being aware that you may be mistaken

doesn't mean merely being aware that you are a fallible human being: it means that you have some concrete reason to suppose that you may be mistaken in this case. Just as "but I may fail" doesn't mean merely "but I am a weak human being" (in which case it would be no more exciting than adding "D.V."): it means that there is some concrete reason for me to suppose that I shall break my word. It is naturally always possible ("humanly" possible) that I may be mistaken or may break my word, but that by itself is no bar against using the expressions "I know" and "I promise" as we do in fact use them.[6]

When we say we *know* something, this presupposes we have no reason to think that any manner of 'special circumstances' hold. Of course, that does not mean that in fact no such circumstance holds. It just means that if one does, we are not aware of it. Nevertheless, to believe that an exact formulation of a knowledge claim should ideally include such a qualification, is simply to miss what knowledge is. To claim knowledge of something is to exclude *any* such possibility. However, on the other hand, it is a consequence of the fact that knowledge (what we usually mean by 'knowledge') constitutes a grasp of externality, that we can never *absolutely* exclude such a possibility. All knowledge requires an unquestioned basis, one in which it is not grounded as knowledge, but that only allows for its meaningful foundation; this basis constitutes the *background* against which knowledge *can* be established and there might be reasons for it. This background only comes to the fore when it is no longer obvious that the conditions on the knowledge we claim to allegedly have are met. In which case, what had not thus far counted as genuine knowledge (e.g., the belief that certain objects disappear and come into being again) can, under the pressure of events, wind up counting as such. However, in each case, to know something is simply to engage with *the externality of what is not as such known, and that constitutes the background of genuine, full-blooded, knowledge.*

6. Austin 1961, p 98.

CHAPTER THREE

De Re Intentionality and the Limits of Interpretation

MAKING IT EXPLICIT (MIE) is undoubtedly unique in the contemporary philosophical landscape. It can be read in many ways, including as an encyclopaedia of Analytic philosophy of language and mind in the last century. It would therefore be surprising if there were nothing to be found in it on the topic of *de re* intentionality. This topic has become quite central in the context of English-speaking philosophy over the last thirty years. Given his systematic ambitions Robert Brandom could not have stopped short of giving an account of it. This is exactly what he does, or tries to do, in the final chapter of the book.

Now, on Brandom's understanding of it, this topic is not simply one among many. It presents a very specific difficulty. This is firstly because the basic framework of *MIE* is characterized by the adoption of a merely *normative* perspective, as opposed to an intentionalist one. This does not mean that Brandom wants to do away with intentionality, but from his standpoint it is not basic. What are basic are our normative achievements, for only they can be the possible objects of *scorekeeping.* Intentional content, instead of being the basis of scorekeeping, must be derived from the process of scorekeeping. Thus, if '*de re* intentionality' is to be thought of as a special instance of 'intentionality,' it is a special case of something relatively superficial, and so unable to play the role of an explanatory principle.

What makes matters worse in the case of '*de re* intentionality' is the fact that the notion seems to draw upon an essentially *representational* sense of intentionality. What seems to be characteristic of *de re* intentionality is the fact that it is essentially intentionality *of* something; as such, it is its representational structure. Indeed, the section of *MIE* that Brandom dedicates to *de re* intentionality is the final one in which we return to the *representational level*. Now, in Brandom's view this level is not fundamental. The essential structure of thought is *inferential* rather than representational. If intentionality (at least from the perspective of how Brandom sets up his question at the very beginning of the book) is merely the surface of thought, then representation is the surface of the surface.

This does not mean that it is unimportant. In fact, it is very important that our thinking possesses representational structure. However, this structure cannot be presupposed, but has to be *recovered:* deduced, in a quasi-Kantian sense of the term, by other means. One must be able to paraphrase this representational structure in a language that is not—that is, not immediately—representational, and then reconstruct this structure *from the outside*. Let us remember this phrase: 'from the outside'—it will prove pivotal. What Brandom proffers in the last chapter of his book is indeed something like *a social deduction of the representational structure of thought*. On such a conception a representation cannot be fundamental, and so its particular structure—being 'of' something—can only be derived from another dimension. We shall call this the *perspectival dimension*—the social dimension of reasoning itself. Against this background the contemporary, merely *semantic*, discussion regarding whether intentionality is *de re* or not, appears ultimately abstract and superficial. Brandom, at least, cannot take it at face value.

Even if such notions cannot any longer be treated as basic, inferentialism nevertheless has the task of recovering them at a derivative level, and of providing some explanation of their apparent value. The problem, however, is that there may be something in the very notion of *de re* intentionality that resists this reconstruction. The notion might turn out to involve too many presuppositions—presuppositions that, as such, are incompatible with the inferentialist perspective as Brandom sets it out. As a matter of fact, *de re* intentionality might even be *the title under which such presuppositions fall*—those that are incompatible with *strong inferentialism*, at least.

Put roughly, the idea of '*de re* intentionality' as it features in the contemporary literature is that of *a relation with an object*. Usually the sorts of theories that put forward the idea of *de re* intentionality adopt a resolutely referential perspective on intentionality (i.e., they are diverse forms of *referentialism*.) Moreover, in these theories it is very common to interpret reference itself as a full-blooded relation to an object that clearly presupposes the object's existence.

Now, Brandom, at the beginning of the second part of his book, makes clear that he questions the very idea of a 'reference-relation':

> Various word-world relations play important explanatory roles in theoretical semantic projects, but to think of any one of these as what is referred to as 'the reference relation' is to be bewitched by surface syntactic form.[1]

This passage suggests that what we might be tempted to treat as a relation is in fact the illusion of a relation—its relational appearance being merely a superficial effect induced by the surface syntactical form.

It seems difficult, on this account, to recover a phenomenon like *de re* intentionality as something genuinely substantial. If there is no such thing as a reference relation it becomes particularly challenging to account for the case in which it is supposed to be *essential* that reference constitutes a relation. Brandom's strategy for tackling this issue is, as usual, ingenious. I am not sure it is absolutely convincing. I have the impression that Brandom's recovery of *de re* intentionality misses something. It is this dissatisfaction I would like to clarify.

Brandom's move—a bold one—consists in shifting the problem from that of *intentionality de re* to that of *ascription de re*. Now, it would

1. Brandom 1994, p. 325.

be misleading to say that this is just another perspective on the same problem, as if the point were to look at *de re* intentionality from the point of view of the activity thinkers engage in when ascribing thoughts to one another. The claim is stronger: *de re* ascriptions are not just a perspective on *de re* intentionality, but the truth of the latter. One could even say that there is, properly speaking, no such thing as *de re* intentionality, or that it is akin to an optical effect resulting from the more fundamental phenomenon of *de re* ascription. Either way, it is the ascription rather than the intentionality itself that is essentially *de re* and it is on the former that the notion of *de re* intentionality in fact depends.

This claim concerns the philosophy of mind, but it is nevertheless based on an observation that pertains to the philosophy of language; as such, it cannot be separated from the idea that it is the linguistic perspective that provides an adequate grasp of mind: the structure of mind is revealed in the manner of its expression (this is the central claim of *expressivism*). Now, at the linguistic level

> *De re* ascriptions are the fundamental representational locution of natural languages.[2]

This entails a complete change of perspective, one that is genuinely exciting. The question however is whether or not it allows us to recover everything usually indicated by the phrase '*de re*.' Is a complete reconstruction possible? If not, perhaps this is because there is something metaphysical in our traditional use of the notion, something it would be preferable give up in favour of Brandom's view. However, as we shall see, there is reason to suspect otherwise. The Brandomian framework comes at too high a price, and the tricks that are required within it in order to make sense of what it excludes are what ultimately seem metaphysical. Indeed, transcendental metaphysics generally consists in retrieving what one has unduly disposed of.

2. Brandom 1994, p. 499.

Brandom makes a strong point in the final chapter of *MIE*:

> The representational dimension of propositional content is con-
> ferred on thought and talk by the *social* dimension of the practice of
> giving and asking for reasons.[3]

This proposition offers an explanation: it points to the origin of the representational structure of thought. That origin is found in the sociality of the game that consists in giving and asking for reasons. Thought is representational *because* it is social. The grounding of what appears to be an essential aspect of thought (its being representational) in its sociality is undoubtedly interesting. The sociality of thought has apparently never been emphasized to this extent.

Two things can be said concerning the structure of the argument. The first is that, exciting as it might be, the motivation for it is somewhat peculiar. After all, it is not clear at all that if thought is representational—which in some sense it certainly is—it is representational for a *reason*. Doesn't this amount to asking *why thought is thought?* It is not at all clear that it makes any sense to ask this question—what could be meant by it?

Secondly, to say that the social nature of thought is what makes thought representational makes it sound as though thought's sociality *does something* to thought—making it something it would otherwise fail to be independent of the transcendental force of sociality that is exerted on it. However, it is unclear how sociality could do anything to thought, for this presupposes that thought could be something (that is, something other than it actually is) independently of it. However, what thought could be independently of its much-vaunted sociality is utterly unclear. What are we talking about by this point? By putting too much emphasis on the so-called sociality of thought it is possible that we end up producing the opposite result to the one we expected.

3. Brandom 1994, p. 426.

What does it mean to say that, according to Brandom, the representational structure of discourse depends essentially on its being social? It means that representation functions as an *ascriptional device.*

At the basic level at which *MIE* has operated until this point, we ascribe intentional contents, that is, beliefs or other such assessable attitudes, to one another through scorekeeping. These contents may be the objects of *de dicto* reports as when, for example, I say that Raoul believes *that that young lady is a spy.* A *de re* report, on the other hand, emphasizes the object of such an attitude. This could be expressed formally as: 'Raoul believes of that harmless student (e.g.) that she is a spy.' We no longer have a global content that one may or may not believe. Rather, the content is specified as being *about a definite object,* one which the report picks out independently of the fact it is the object of a belief.

The interpretation Brandom gives of this difference is very convincing: if reference to the object has been isolated and so to speak 'subtracted' from the assessable content itself, it no longer belongs to the same perspective. Two perspectives are featured in the sentence: an external one—the speaker's—according to which the object is a harmless student; and that of Raoul, who takes her to be a spy. Brandom's idea is that there is no reference to an object (no 'representation') independently of the contrast between different perspectives. The 'object' as such is essentially a perspectival device.

The same sort of contrast can be found between what an agent tries to do and what he succeeds in doing.[4] In general, it seems that for Brandom the object is at the 'intersection' of the first and third person. This idea is not so novel. However, Brandom's treatment of it has an unprecedented depth. It is not that the object could be seen (differently) from a first-person *and* a third-person perspective— as if it existed independently of those viewpoints and preceded them. The object is *nothing but the articulation of this difference in*

---

4. See Brandom 1994, p. 522.

perspective: the function of the particle 'of' is just to establish the contrast between the perspective of one undertaking a commitment and of one assessing it. Thus, intersubjectivity—or more precisely, *sociality,* given that it is essential that the 'external' view of the commitment is in the *third* person, not just *another first person*—is not merely a precondition on the appearance of objectivity, but the substance of objectivity itself.

This is a bold and interesting view. One could even say that the sociality of thought has never been upheld in such a radical manner. However, even putting to one side questions concerning whether this move—that of making thought entirely social—is necessary, perhaps the kind of 'dialogical' objectivity it leaves us with is *phenomenologically* unsatisfactory. Perhaps we have made full sense of *objectivity* this way. But *have we not simultaneously lost the sense of the object,* that which the majority of contemporary semantic analyses are responding to?

It is particularly interesting to consider the particular analyses Brandom gives of contemporary discussions concerning *de re* intentionality in both semantics and the philosophy of mind from this perspective. The very phenomenon of *de re* belief seems difficult, if not impossible, to capture within the Brandomian framework, for its expression seems to rest on the very notion of 'denotation' that Brandom, in his previous analyses, has called into question.

What is a *de re* belief? Borrowing Tyler Burge's analysis,[5] we can say that

S believes$_R$ of t that $\varphi(t)$
iff
S believes$_N$ $\varphi(\alpha)$ and α denotes t

(using believes$_R$ for 'believes *de re*,' and believes$_N$ for 'believes notionally'). So, a *de re* belief can be explained in terms of a notional belief *plus* the specification of a denotation. Brandom gets around

5. Brandom 1994, p. 548sq.

this difficulty by resorting to the strategy he has already introduced. This consists in substituting the notion of substitutional commitment for the relation of denotation. Saying that α denotes t is a matter of indicating what may be substituted for α whilst preserving the inferential value of the content in which it occurs. Thus, the determination of denotation remains immanent to the normative game. On this understanding, the recasting of the notion of *de re* belief in inferentialist terms does not raise any particular difficulties.

It seems, however, that what Brandom calls *de re* belief "in the epistemically strong sense" may be different. In a striking summary of the debates in the philosophy of language since the 1970s he writes:

> In the seventies Burge, Perry, Lewis, and Kaplan himself, among others, focus attention on the kind of beliefs that are *de re* or relational in the epistemically strong sense that results from insisting that the believer be in a position to pick out the object of belief by the use of demonstratives or, more generally, indexical expressions.[6]

And, quite correctly, he says:

> Since that time much effort has been invested in the notion that 'directly referential' expressions, paradigmatically indexical ones, make possible a fundamental sort of contact with the objects of thought, a kind of relational belief that is not conceptually mediated—in which objects are directly present to the mind, rather than being presented by the use of concepts.[7]

Against theories of 'direct reference' Brandom emphasizes the conceptual nature of demonstrative reference. Demonstration has the function of establishing reference only insofar as it is a genuine move in a normative scorekeeping game and is thus *conceptual.*

---

6. Brandom 1994, p. 551.
7. Brandom 1994, p. 551.

To this extent I think Brandon is correct. Demonstration is not a confrontation with a mere datum. It is a way of articulating a grip on an object, one which opens up space for an assessment. There are certainly *demonstrative concepts*. My reluctance does not concern Brandom's conceptualism (or what we could more correctly call his 'anti-non-conceptualism': on Brandom's view concepts do not play a grounding role—this is performed by *reasonings*).

What I feel uneasy about is Brandom's *minimalism*. He insists that he does not buy into any of the views about the nature of the alleged relation between belief and its object in the case of the 'epistemically strong *de re* belief.' The formal framework he forwards for *de re* mental states is supposed to be compatible with one or another interpretation (weak or strong) of this alleged relation. The problem is that Brandom's minimalism seems to be incompatible with the 'strong' interpretation of '*de re*' states—the 'object-dependence' interpretation. Brandom often insists that his theory takes the *de dicto / de re* distinction seriously—and it undoubtedly does. In his framework, the characterization of a *de re* state makes a difference— a logical difference in the extended sense of the word 'logic' that is characteristic of *MIE*. The question is whether this is enough.

From the point of view of those theories that since the 1970s have advanced the notion of object-dependent meaning (not to be confused with the notion of 'direct reference' which does without meaning), it is doubtful that it is enough. In their view a full-blooded relation is not optional, nor is it enough that the formal framework we adopt *allows* it. Instead our semantics must *presuppose* it as the basis for at least some of our meanings. The strong interpretation of the relation is not optional but fundamental. The simple fact that Brandom presents that possibility as one among others is by itself highly suspicious: dealt with on his terms, the notion of object-dependence threatens to become anaemic.

I can certainly ascribe a relation a speaker bears to an object. However, on the object-dependence conception, the meaning of the speaker's terms will be constituted by the fact that she *has* that relation to the object. The relation is not only something that might be *ascribed*, but something that can be *entertained*, and it is essential that it is sometimes entertained *effectively*.

Brandom's analysis of how it is possible to include a demonstrative reference in an anaphoric one is undoubtedly illuminating. He is definitely onto something here, for it is most likely correct that an essential aspect of demonstrative reference is that it can be taken up in this way. Demonstrative reference is not isolated. It only makes sense as a form of reference insofar as it participates in what we might call the 'game of reference'—that is to say, only insofar as questions can be asked concerning *what is referred to* by an act of singular reference.

However, Brandom writes that:

> It is *only* as initiators of anaphoric chains that demonstrative and indexical tokenings provide ways of talking and thinking about objects at all, and hence potentially as *strongly* of or about them.[8]

This sounds excessively *reductive:* it is as though the possibility of being included in anaphoric reference is what bears the entire referential burden in demonstrative reference. Instead, why not acknowledge the *solidarity* that exists between demonstrative and other kinds of reference, while simultaneously making anaphoric reference a privileged partner?

In this regard, Brandom's discussion of John McDowell's position in the section dedicated to 'epistemically strong *de re* attitudes,' is particularly interesting.[9] In 'De Re senses,'[10] McDowell criticizes the metaphor according to which thoughts are to be 'shared' and where communication consists in sharing such thoughts. Following in Gareth Evans's footsteps, he considers Gottlob Frege's famous claim that 'I' means something particular to each speaker, so that, using this word, she can express thoughts that another person could

8. Brandom 1994, p. 573.
9. Brandom 1994, p. 562.
10. McDowell 1984.

not express or entertain. However, McDowell says that another person can entertain and express thoughts that are 'in a suitable relation of correspondence' to the ones I express using the first person. Whenever I say 'I am sad,' you can say 'you are sad.' This does not express the same thought, but it does at least express *a corresponding thought*—a thought that *constitutively* corresponds to mine.

McDowell's point is quite Strawsonian. The idea is that there is an essential solidarity between the language game of the first person and that of the second (and third) person. This does not amount to the claim that what is said in the first person could be said, without remainder, in the second or third person. There is something irreducible about the first-person perspective: some things can *only* be said in the first person. However, when something can be said using the first person, there is, correlatively, something to be said either in the second or third person (something else, but still something 'corresponding' to the first-person thought). This is a point about the language game of the various persons—and of what can be said in a 'personal' way.

It is easy to see how far this analysis is from Brandom's. There is no story here about the necessary take-up of real indicators (in the first person) as 'quasi-indicators' (in the third person). McDowell's point more concerns the *a priori* correlation between indicators (or of indicators with devices that are not themselves indicators but work at the same level as indicators). The point is not to *emulate* an act of reference that only someone else can achieve (because it concerns them or something nearby in their environment), but to adopt *the corresponding form of reference*. Of course, this presupposes that there are connections between the concepts of the first, second, and third person from the outset.

We are getting close to the core issue now: McDowell's account involves a full recognition of the first-person perspective. It brings out the essential connection between this perspective and that of the second and third persons—connections that do not entail a reduction of the first to the second and third. On the contrary, the first person belongs to a *system of persons*. As such it is irreducible. Brandom, on the other hand, adopts the third-person perspective throughout his analysis. The first-person point of view is not denied so much as it is *recovered from outside*, treated as something that is not significant in its own right.

This judgment may seem harsh, as Brandom continually says that his perspective is not so much a third-person one—if by this one means the perspective of the *they* (i.e., the third person plural). It is an *I-thou* perspective: a *dialogical perspective*. This is because the difference between *status* and *attitude*—objective content and a subjective perspective on it—is found only *in the relation between two people*. The problem is that Brandom's conception of dialogue and the I-thou relation is essentially third-personal. It is as if each were *the observer* of the other's performance and had to assess it from 'outside,' so to speak. In a process of communication conceived of as a perpetual activity of scorekeeping, each of us becomes an umpire, or plays the part of both umpire and player *alternatively*.

This conception of thought and communication seems to me to be deeply misguided. In the first part of his book Brandom follows in Wittgenstein's footsteps by rejecting the characterization of our relation to rules as one of 'interpretation' (even if he blunts Wittgenstein's point by confusing what lies beneath any interpretation with the idea of what is *implicit*, and so with that can be made explicit). Yet in the final part of this book he is irresistibly drawn to the concept of interpretation precisely at the point at which the content of thought is at stake. Rules cannot be objects of interpretation all the way down, but our *claims* essentially are insofar as they constitute the ordinary substance of thought:

> Propositional, and so conceptual, *understanding* is rooted in the *interpretation* that *communication* requires, rooted in the *social* practice of deontic *scorekeeping*.[11]

11. Brandom 1994, p. 517.

The reduction of understanding to interpretation is questionable. It is not at all clear that understanding something, for example an utterance, is always a matter of 'interpreting' it. And what should we say about *our own words*, which at least on some occasions we do understand? It would be strange to say we interpret those. We are not, in the first instance, *interpreters* of ourselves. Probably not of others either, at least not systematically.

This remark opens up a gap between Brandom's perspective and that of philosophers like Evans or McDowell who resolutely adopt the perspective of *understanding*—one that is not solipsistic or monological, but according to which the subject is the real locus of truth. For instance, consider once again the switch between first-person and second-person perspectives, as shown in *The Twelve Labours of Asterix:*

- Repeat after me: 'I am a wild boar, I am a wild boar'
- You are a wild boar, you are a wild boar!

Brandom would speak of an *interpretation* here:

> Communication is still possible, but it essentially involves intralinguistic *interpretation*—the capacity to accommodate differences in discursive perspective, to navigate across them.[12]

However, except in some cases, no interpretation is involved in the simple *correlation* of 'I' and 'Thou'—'I' is essentially the 'Thou' of the other. Perhaps a switch of perspective is involved, but the special link between these perspectives is part of the meaning of the word 'I.' It is not that, as Brandom would put it, it *takes on* this meaning from outside; that it correlates with the meaning of 'Thou' is an aspect of its *own* meaning.

In fact, Brandom clings to the traditional conception of conceptual or propositional contents because he thinks that *they can genuinely be shared*. But he thinks the price of their being shared is always an interpretation: we cannot just pass "something non

12. Brandom 1994, p. 588.

perspectival from hand to hand (or mouth to mouth)," we constantly have to translate from one perspective into another.[13] McDowell, on the other hand, takes the notion of 'thought sharing' to be a bad metaphor. The same thought does not need to be expressed in the various different perspectives that it is translated into or out of. This quest for intertranslatability is senseless simply because it is point-less. More important is the fact that our thoughts, or at least some of them, are of a *personal character;* they answer each other, one person to another. Conceptual contents are not monological—*but only be-cause thought itself is not monological*—not because dialogue (i.e., the switch of perspective) *does* anything to it. No (transcendental) deduction of the personal character of thought is required, since thought already *is* intrinsically personal.

According to Brandom:

> Reidentifying conceptual contents through shifts in doxastic and practical point of view requires *interpretation*—substituting one ex-pression of a claim for another.[14]

It is highly questionable whether the basic cases Brandom considers—that is, the switch from the first person to the second—must, nor-mally, involve any interpretation. Of course, things change as the content of thought becomes progressively more complicated. How-ever, that which can be correctly described as the essential intersub-jectivity of thought is not primarily *interpretative:* it is a structure of thought itself insofar as it is *our* thought—and what else could thought be?

Nevertheless, our criticism of Brandom's *hermeneutical* stance may seem unjust insofar as he takes care to distinguish between undertaking a commitment and attributing one:

> Undertaking a commitment is to be distinguished from attributing it to oneself, which is only one species of that attitude.[15]

---

13. Brandom 1994, p. 590.
14. Brandom 1994, p. 591.
15. Brandom 1994, p. 596.

In the standard situation I do not attribute commitments to myself, I undertake them. The latter doesn't require the former. There is, therefore, a real asymmetry between the first- and third-person points of view. Brandom's whole analysis rests on this asymmetry— one which opens up space for representation considered as *the logical locus of the difference between perspectives.*

However, although undertaking is not the same as attributing, the problem is that:

> Attribution can be seen to be the fundamental deontic attitude. Undertaking commitments can be understood in terms of attributing them if the social articulation of scorekeeping attributions is kept in mind: an interlocutor can count as having undertaken a commitment (as being committed) whenever others are entitled—to attribute that commitment.[16]

Therefore, once pride of place has been given to the *social articulation* of attribution, undertaking a commitment can be analysed in terms of attributing one. And these attributions are themselves understood systematically in terms of 'interpretation' as they concern *claims.* Thought, therefore, is always already understood from the point of view of *translation.* Indeed, in the final part of *MIE* there are recognisable traces of Donald Davidson's approach.

Now, it is not at all clear that this account captures the phenomena it claims to. If the same thought can be expressed in diverse ways depending on the speaker's perspective, and if translations between them are possible, still, *that does not mean the articulation of the thought depends in any way on these translations.* My thought is about what it is about independently of your capacity to identify its object correctly—even in the case where I myself am mistaken about the object of my thought.

Raoul might believe that this harmless student is a spy, but his thought is no less about her, even if he is mistaken as to her real identity. Furthermore, my external perspective is not required in order to make it such that his thought is, objectively, about her: genuine

16. Brandom 1994, p. 596.

'aboutness' is an internal feature of his thought, the essential relation that makes it the thought it is. This means that no form of *external* sociality, something additional to the thinker himself, is required in order to open his thought up to the world. His thought, as thought, is immediately in touch with things and thus stands alongside your thought and mine. Thought is not public because it is social—rather, it is social because it is public—and *this publicity, as such, includes sociality as part of itself:* thinking about the world brings with it the risk that other thinking agents do not think the same things you do about objects which are nonetheless the same.

We cannot simply remain at the third-person point of view. There is a legitimacy to the first person and although it is not the whole of thought, it is nonetheless an irreducible aspect of it and should not be analysed merely from the outside. The space of thought is completely determined by the fact that *all of us are 'first persons':* that is to say, each of us is in contact with things themselves and even if we do not have the same relation to them as our neighbours, (1) still, we are related to them, (2) moreover, very often there is a correlation— which is not the same as a translation—between these relations. Thus, *living-together-in-a-world* may prove to be more important to thought itself—*not only as its tacit background, but as part of its very content*—than *constructing that world together* through reciprocal interpretation. From this perspective, the form of semantic 're- alism' that Brandom claims to inherit from Frege sounds quite fantastic. Under the pretence of grounding thoughts in reality, it seems merely to have created an incredible distance between them.

Brandom favours Frege's tactile metaphor of grasping. This metaphor certainly suggests some kind of contact, and, in Brandom's mind at least, it is supposed to. However, what do we grasp according to him? In his view:

> One can grasp an anaphoric chain as one grasps a stick; direct contact is achieved only with one end of it, and there may be much about what is beyond that direct contact of which one is unaware.[17]

17. Brandom 1994, p. 583.

No doubt:

> direct contact with one end gives genuine if indirect contact with
> what is attached to the other end.[18]

However, so we wind up in a strange situation: *we are like blind
people touching objects with the very end of their sticks.*
    Brandom writes that:

> The Cartesian model of conceptual contents restricts them to the part
> of the stick touching one's hand, at the cost of mystery about how our
> cognitive reach can exceed that immediate grasp. A *tactile* Fregean
> semantic theory, of the sort epitomized by understanding proper
> names as constellations of singular-term tokenings articulated by ana-
> phoric commitments, effaces this impermeable boundary between the
> transparency of the mind and the opacity of its objects.[19]

He is certainly right about the limitations of a strict "Cartesian"
model (this might be a straw man, but I won't polemicize here).
Firstly, however, it might so happen that the hand does not touch the
stick, but the thing itself (and without the aid of a stick). Secondly, it
often happens that several hands are touching the very same 'thing':
we do not think alone—*we think together*—in diverse but related
ways. Thirdly, in the very operations by which we manipulate the
anaphoric chains Brandom describes so well, we still remain in contact with many things (not just the ends of the chains) which other
people may also be in contact with in various ways that are corre-
lated to ours. Even *if we sometimes use sticks to get at things, we
and everyone else are still amidst the things themselves.*
    The world is more than the score kept in our language games. It
is their *scene*, as well that of much else that it makes no sense to
describe as 'games,' but which still belong to thought. *We think in*
the world.

18. Brandom 1994, p. 583.
19. Brandom 1994, p. 583.

CHAPTER FOUR

On the Very Idea of 'Phenomenal Content'

If ANYTHING has 'phenomenal content,' then surely perception does. Perception is something you *feel*. It is unclear what it would be to perceive without feeling. In every perception there is apparently something that is intrinsically conscious.

However, perhaps the idea of 'unconscious perception' makes some sense. This issue is connected with (1) the possibility of a merely *intentional* determination of perception and (2) the question whether intentionality is first-personally conscious or not. It might be the case that content should be ascribed to a particular perceptual state of which the perceiver is unaware. The question is what qualifies this state as one of 'perception.' On a purely functional definition of perception, according to which perception is access to information that can play a causal role in our behaviour, phenomenal consciousness *("feel")* does not seem necessary. From this point of view, subliminal perception is still a perception. However, does this hold for the paradigm case of what we *ordinarily* call 'perception'? Do we not call the ordinary case 'perception' because there is some experience, one which presupposes and involves a phenomenal consciousness that we normally call 'perception'? We can at least say that, in some basic sense of the word, perception is conscious perception. For any given perception, *there is something it is like to have it.*

I do not say: for any given 'perception *of something*'—that is, a definite thing—there is something it is like to have it. To do so would be to take it for granted that there is a bi-univocal correspondence between the identification of perception by its *phenomenal character* ('the way it feels') and the identification of perception by its *intentional content*. In so doing, we would have assumed that this problem is already solved.

What is clear at the outset is in fact a far more limited point: that perception, in some canonical sense of the term, is a kind of *experience*, and thus *there is something it is like* to have it. From this point of view, whether one perceives makes a difference. Taking up John Locke's example we can say that representing a pineapple, perhaps because you read a description of it in a travel book, is not the same as tasting it. In tasting it you perceive it and, in so doing, enjoy an experience.

'Experience,' at least here, is *something you have*. There is no experience that you do not 'have.' There is at most *the representation of an experience*. For the time being we should leave open the question whether such representation—and perhaps *representation* in general—involves an experience of its own. Whether or not, that is, there is something it is like *to represent*—perhaps even to represent a particular thing. Even in this case the so-called experience of representing should not be confused with the represented experience. Actually experiencing something is somehow *sui generis*.

If this is what the notion of 'phenomenal content' comes down to, perhaps we should acknowledge it. However, the *qualitative dimension of 'having an experience'* is perhaps better captured by what philosophers call 'phenomenal character.' For in saying that there is something irreducible about having a definite perceptual experience, we have so far said nothing that suggests that this experience has a 'content'—a notion to be defined—let alone that this content is 'phenomenal.' On the other hand, as intuitive as the idea of 'phenomenal character' might seem, I am not sure that we should be content with it. There is nothing wrong, I think, with the idea that there is *something it is like* to have an experience. On some understanding of this expression ('what it is like to'), it is just part of experience's *definition*. But why should this involve a story about 'phenomenality'?

'Phenomenal,' etymologically and philosophically, means *appearing*. Why should we describe experience as 'appearing'? As, that is, appearing *to* someone, *to* a subject, as is logically required by the syntax of the verb? This turn of phrase, familiar though it may be within a certain philosophical tradition, nonetheless sounds strange. According to the regular syntax of 'experience,' our 'experiences' do not 'appear' to us. We *have* them, in a way that requires the progressive form: 'I am having an experience.' A kind of direct transitivity seems to be involved: an *internal accusative*. As a matter of fact, experience just is its 'being had.'

Doesn't talk of experience 'appearing'—or to put it in technical terms, its 'phenomenality'—already create a gap between an *experience* and *its being had* that cannot exist? I would be inclined to say that an experience does not appear; it just *is* what it is. Or, more precisely, it 'appears' insofar as we place it in an intentional scenario. Let us imagine that I have never tasted a pineapple. "Here is one," I say, "I will try it and see how it tastes." Perhaps in these circumstances an experience might be said to 'appear'—for now it is given, and can either accord with or run contrary to my expectations. However, can we really say it is 'given' or that it 'appears' by itself, independently of this network of expectations and other intentional attitudes? The philosophical way of speaking that moves from talk of this kind to 'appearing' in general seems strange somehow.

To say that 'experiences,' in particular perceptual ones, have a 'phenomenal character' suggests, paradoxically, that experiences could be what they are independently of the fact that they 'appear.' However, in the sense in which people who say that experiences 'appear' mean, experiences are nothing independently of their 'appearing'—and so one loses sight of the point of saying that experiences 'appear' and have 'a phenomenal character.' *For what is appearing opposed to here?* Perhaps experiences are 'subjective,' and so do not comprise that which belongs to the objects themselves independently of the subject's experience of them? In this sense—that is, in contrast to what is 'objective'—experiences might be said to 'appear,' insofar as *their being is that of being for a subject.*

In response to this conception, which is typical of modern philosophy, we should perhaps say that the basis, or at least one basis, of the notion of a subject for which experiences are supposed to be 'appearances,' is found *in the concept of experience.* As such the direction of conceptual dependence is in fact the reverse of what it seems. Experiences set the standard for phenomenality, and so it does not make sense to call *them* 'phenomenal.' They are no more 'phenomenal' than the subject is 'subjective.' Of course, there is another way—perhaps not unrelated—of making sense of so-called 'phenomenality.' That is to *consider every experience as the manifestation* of *something.* Experiences do not 'appear,' but they are intrinsically *appearances of something.* The 'phenomenal character' of experience can then be contrasted with the mere objectivity of what is referred to. What appears is not the experience, but the object.

In order to preserve the phrase 'what it is like to' we should say that an experience can be, for example, *what it is like to see a red apple* or perhaps, in order to provisionally avoid the problem of the *range* of so-called 'phenomenal properties,' *what it is like to see a red object.* Of course, one cannot rule out the possibility that what it is like to see a red object could also be correctly described in different terms, such as *what it is like to see an object with a warmer colour than green,* etc. Such descriptions need not *uniquely* describe any given kind of experience. What matters is that, in general, they can *adequately* describe an experience. On this understanding we have *experiences of things* or particular qualities of them ("Have you ever experienced the taste of the durian?"). In such experiences things or aspects of things 'appear.' However, they appear in *a particular way:* with a certain 'phenomenal character.'

It is far from certain that this philosophical description of experience as 'the *appearance* of something'—I mean: of something different from itself—is correct. It might turn out to depend on very strong—and questionable—assumptions.

Is it not true that the language game of 'experience' includes the possibility of the *external transitivity of experience:* not merely experience, but 'experience of'? It seems to make sense to describe an experience as 'what it is like *to see something yellow.*' It makes sense precisely because perception is a form of experience. Therefore, perception provides a format—an intentional one, insofar as to perceive is to perceive *some particular thing*—according to which at least some experiences are characterized.

Not all experiences, however. Going under the dentist's drill is certainly an experience. How can something we 'mind' so much not be? Furthermore it is very specific. Speaking about it vividly reminds you of it. However, in spite of the acute specificity of this experience, it is difficult to describe it as the experience 'of' the dentist's drill as an object. This experience is not exactly perceptual—it hurts too much for that. As such we should not describe this experience as what it is like to *perceive* the dentist's drill, but as what it is like *to suffer it.* Shall we say that this situation, which includes us as an intimate part of it, 'appears' to us?

Some experiences can be described as 'experiences of something,' others not. Should we assume that the latter constitute the basis for the others, something like a primitive form of experience that can grow, turning into 'the appearing of something'? First you have to feel it, and only later can it become 'the feeling *of* something.' This development, assuming it made sense, would explain why we talk of *appearing* in relation to experience: from the 'mere appearance' that has not yet been identified as 'of something'—but that is still something in its own right—to the 'same' appearance understood as being *of* what is. It would be as if I could be trained to *perceive*—rather than merely suffer—the dentist's drill.

I take this position to be mistaken. It rests on an oversimplification of the grammar of experience, treating it as though every experience were teleologically oriented toward the kind of experience which can be described in intentional terms. This particular kind of experience then sets the standard for experience in general. According to this standard, the supposedly 'simple' non-intentional experience is still an *appearing*—even if *we do not know what, apart from itself, it's an appearance of*. As such, the self-appearing of experience—which is usually taken to characterize 'phenomenal consciousness'—is a privative version of full-blooded appearing, the appearing of an object: *intentional* appearing, in other words.

This view does not accommodate the genuine diversity that exists within the grammar of experience. Since the syntax of experience is far from uniform, we should not reduce its diversity too hastily by saying that 'every experience is an experience *of* something'—or is on its way to becoming one. One kind of experience is not 'the same as the other, only 'more primitive.' Nor is it a *part* of the other. *It is simply something else.* The concept of experience is as rich as all the things *we call 'experiences' and which we characterize in very different ways.*

This grammatical point does not abolish the unity of the concept of experience, because all the things we call experience are ways 'it is like' to do something or be in certain situations. Nonetheless, they are not all describable as consciousness of an object—which is not to say that some of them are more *elementary* than, or merely a part of, that kind of consciousness. They are simply *something different*, but despite that they are still experiences, even if they differ in kind from consciousness of an object. That does not mean that they have no syntax, that there is no way of characterizing them. However, characterizing them involves reference to *the kinds of occasion on which one has them*. This is a perfectly correct way to characterize *some* experiences.

As a matter of fact, reducing the grammar of experience to a univocal form—the intentional form—is characteristic of what we can call the *perceptual model of experience*. According to it every experience is an 'experience of' something in the sense in which perception is 'perception of' something. It makes good sense to describe some 'experiences' as 'perception'—others not. Now, calling an experience an 'appearance of something' is appropriate precisely insofar as the experience can be described as a perception. Thus, perception seems to be the key to 'appearing.' However, this presupposes, perhaps hastily, that talk of 'appearing' is appropriate when applied to perception.

Now, as Aristotle notes, "usually, when sense functions accurately in regard to the sensible object, we do not say that *this appears to us a human being,* but rather when we cannot clearly perceive whether he / she is a true or false human being." (οὐδὲ λέγομεν, ὅταν ἐνεργῶμεν ἀκριβῶς περὶ τὸ αἰσθητόν, **ὅτι φαίνεται τοῦτο ἡμῖν ἄνθρωπος,** ἀλλὰ μᾶλλον ὅταν μὴ ἐναργῶς αἰσθανώμεθα πότερον ἀληθὴς ἢ ψευδής.)[1]

Thus, successful acts of perception do not call for talk of 'appearing' (φαίνεσθαι) per se. This is only appropriate when, for whatever reason, doubts arise about *what* we perceive. In a normal situation, we do not say that what we see *appears to us* as this or that. We just say that we see it. And, in saying so, we assume that we see things as they are—not as they 'appear.' There is no reason to talk as though perception *in general* deals with 'appearings'; genuine acts of perception deal only with reality. This is how the verbs of perception work:

"I've seen Nessie."

"No, you've only *seen* a sail in the fog."

Perception, therefore, is probably not the best case to consider if we want to grasp the phenomenality of experience. The fact that we describe perception in an essentially intentional idiom—as 'perception of'—does not necessarily mean that we should buy into a phenomenalist interpretation of this idiom by translating it into talk of the 'appearing of' something.

Roughly speaking then, I am willing to acknowledge that experience in general and perception in particular have a 'character,' that is, some irreducibly qualitative dimension. But I cannot see the point in calling it 'phenomenal.' Once again, if the point is that you *feel* it,

1. *On the Soul,* III, 3, 428a 13–14. I give my own translation, as literal as possible, because the usual translations miss this fine point about the grammar of appearing.

then that's fine. But why should we bring 'phenomenality' into this story? Doing so introduces a very complicated construction—the modern metaphysics of 'subjectivity'—in order to deal with a very simple fact. *Your pain is not phenomenal.* You feel it, and it is *real.* It does not 'appear,' it *is.*

In light of the above, one might expect me to be even more sceptical—for reasons pertaining to the grammar of appearing—of 'phenomenal content.' In fact I have already broached the issue, since these problems are far more intertwined than people generally think. As we have seen, it is very difficult to make sense of the kind of 'phenomenality' that is ascribed to perception as well as experience more generally, except via the potential phenomenality of its *content* (or some part of its content). In fact, it is possible that one upshot of talk of 'phenomenal character' is the temptation to think of that character as itself a kind of 'content,' or else as something intrinsically connected to the disclosure of such content. Thus, in order to explore the grammar of experience in greater depth, we need to take a closer look at the notion of 'phenomenal content.'

The basic issue that needs to be addressed is the meaning of 'content' in this context. It seems there are two possibilities. On the one hand, 'content' might mean, as it does elsewhere, *truth-bearing content*, namely *something that can be said to be true or false.* If so, calling content 'phenomenal' simply places a constraint on its scope, though it nevertheless remains the 'ordinary' sort of content. If by 'content of perception' we mean whatever we can ascribe to an object non-inferentially on the basis of perception (correctly or otherwise), then 'phenomenal' content is that part of the total content that is *really experienced.* (Assuming, that is, that I understand the friends of 'phenomenal content' correctly.) This part of the content is, as such, true or false.

The alternative definition takes phenomenal content to be a different kind of content altogether, a kind which differs from the sort usually thought to be perceptual insofar as it is *neither true nor false.* Thus, 'phenomenal content' is no longer the part of 'the content' of an experience (e.g., perception)—the part that really 'appears' in an experience—but is instead what *really appears in it,* as opposed to its 'content.' The emphasis is on the reality of this appearance ('what *really* appears')—not on any claim to truth that is constitutive of this 'content' as such. However, it seems the mere reality of a given 'appearance' can still justify claims: that is to say, it is undoubtedly true that this 'content,' in a non-alethic sense of the term 'content,' *appears.*

According to the first conception, the concept of phenomenality is a restriction on a predetermined notion of 'content.' According to the second conception, it establishes an original notion of 'content.' Let us develop the first hypothesis. It seems reasonable to think that part of what defines perception is its having 'content.' If you ask me how I can say that Charles is with us, I suppose I can answer: because I see him. Our perceptions can be reasons. This is an important part of the language game of perception. From this point of view it makes sense to ascribe 'contents' to our perceptions.

However, one can object: do you *really* see Charles? Or do you not rather see some shape that you identify as Charles's thanks to some kind of recognition? What really 'appears' to you is not Charles, it is this shape. Thus, one can analyse the content into a part that is 'phenomenal' and a part that is not. Being 'Charles's' is not a phenomenal aspect of the shape. We should distinguish, therefore, between what *is really given* in perception and *what is not.*

Note that, on this conception, what is 'really given' does not necessarily have to be true. Imagine that I have recently been prescribed progressive lenses and as a consequence am having some trouble assessing the depth of steps in a staircase. The way they look to me is part of my perceiving them. However, my perception is misleading, and, if I rely on it, I'll end up being mistaken.

What matters is the contrast between the phenomenal part of the content and the content as a whole. It is tempting to say the following: the contrast in question is between what we *really* see and what we *truly* see. For example, what do I *truly* see when I look at Charles? I suppose the best thing to say is: 'Charles.' That is to say, on the basis of this perceptual episode, I take this thing to be Charles—and I am right, it's *true* that it's Charles. In fact, it would sound quite peculiar to say that I see colour patches, or only a shape that looks like Charles (Charles's 'phenomenal identity'?). At the very least some quite particular circumstances would be required for my saying so to be considered relevant. Let us therefore say that 'Charles' is the 'ordinary' description of what I am seeing.

However, the friends of 'phenomenal content' could say that even if Charles is what I *truly* see, he is nevertheless not what I *really* see. What is *really* given, is just a collection of colour patches or, at best, a shape. Now, in this context, I necessarily apply the concept 'Charles' to this collection of colour patches. The full-blooded 'content' of my perception—the intentional content—is thereby constructed. However, this content includes as part of itself some 'phenomenal content,' otherwise it would not be the intentional content *of a perception*. On this view, what I really see is a part of what I truly see. It is true that I see Charles, but a *real* part of my seeing Charles is my seeing his shape—and so it is also true that I see his shape.

Now, the notion of 'phenomenal content' so understood can—from an epistemological point of view—be used in two different ways. Firstly, it can play the role of something that is known with certainty—as opposed to the intentional content as a whole, which may turn out to be false. For instance, I could say that I have seen Charles, and then qualify this statement by saying that I have seen a man who had his shape. I could then further qualify it by saying that I have only seen something that had his shape. By retreating to the phenomenal aspect of the content I finally appear to be able to say something certain. This does not mean that my initial statement was not true, not a good characterization of what I had seen—*the perceived as such*—the point is merely that what I saw was not *absolutely* certain. Thus, according to this conception, phenomenal content is the *indubitable* aspect of what is perceived.

A second interpretation of 'phenomenal content,' which is quite opposed to the first, understands it to be the merely *ostensible* content of a given perception: that which *seems* to be true without necessarily being the case. Furthermore, in having such a perception one does not necessarily have to consider its content to be true—the Sears tower can seem close by when, in fact, I know that it isn't. As a consequence *I do not see it as being close by*, and without having to make any inference to that effect. Perhaps this example is not entirely convincing. To be frank, I find it very difficult to make sense of this notion of 'phenomenal content.' I know that some philosophers are inclined to say that the stick in the water still *seems* bent even when we know it is straight. But who buys that? No doubt the stick does not look like a straight stick *usually* does when it is out of the water. Yet for all that, does it *seem bent?*

In fact, it is very difficult to understand how perception's 'phenomenal content' could conflict with its 'intentional content.' Indeed, it is possible for things to seem a certain way when in fact they are otherwise, in which case one's perception is misleading. Imagine I am looking at the ceiling of Sant'Ignazio in Rome. *Trompe-l'œil* is all about creating misleading perceptions. If asked, I would say that the church has a vaulted ceiling, when in fact the ceiling is flat and painted with frescoes. Someone could tell me that in fact there is no vault—only ingenious frescoes. If they did, could I still say afterward that *I see the vault?* As a matter of fact, my knowing that there's no vault makes no difference to my perception. In order to *see* what is the case, I need to step a little further into the nave. Then I see the real situation. But this is *another perception:* I cannot ascribe the intentional content of the latter—that is, the claim immediately grounded in it—to the former.

However, can't I in some contexts perceive something that is incompatible with the 'phenomenal content' of that very perception? As when, for example, I see that the ceiling is white, but because of the dim light it 'really' appears to be yellow? The problem is that this is just what 'white' looks like in dim light. It cannot really be said, therefore, that on the level of phenomenal content I take the ceiling to be yellow, and on the level of intentional content I take it to be white. *I just see it as white.* This is contingent, however, on what standard of whiteness I use to characterize what I perceive in this particular situation. A photographer, for example, may decide the very same ceiling will not serve as a white background. That does not mean that there is another content behind or below the one according to which the ceiling is white with which the original content is in conflict. It is simply a consequence of the fact that the characterization of perceptual content is highly contextual. There are not different levels of content in conflict with one another within a single perception. Rather, we should say that any given perception lacks a univocal content. The content of a perception should be assessed differently depending on what epistemic role it plays.

Consequently, there is no room for what merely *seems* to us to be the case in a given perception, where that is opposed to what we perceive (or think we perceive) in it. If in a given perception something really seems to us to be the case, then this is just what we perceive. Or, at least, what we think we perceive—for we might want to question the idea that *perceiving what is not the case* is really *perceiving.* Can I say that I perceive the vault of Sant'Ignazio? Or should I not say that, on the basis of what I perceive—which is not a vault—I believe that there is a vault up there? Perhaps the vault is 'phenomenal' in the sense that it is not real. But what is 'phenomenal' here, is it the intentional object of my perception, or the (false) belief that is based on this perception? In this case, the 'phenomenal' content just *is* the intentional content. You cannot, in general, contrast the 'phenomenal content' of a perception with its intentional content, since to do so is to intentionalize the former, and to intentionalize the former is to make it a part—or the whole—of the latter.

Now, another possibility is that 'phenomenal content' is a distinctive aspect of intentional content: *what 'really appears.'* Once again, we are supposed to draw a distinction within what is 'seen' between what we *really* see and what we claim to see but in fact cannot. Accordingly, we should say that I cannot *really* see Charles, but only his shape. Or, more precisely: a shape. Charles's shape is the phenomenal aspect of Charles, and this shape is the phenomenal content of my perception of Charles.

There are two difficulties we must consider here. Firstly, observe that I would not normally say that I see Charles's shape, but rather that I see Charles. Only in certain circumstances would I say that I see his shape, and if I were to say this, it would be in contrast to 'seeing him.' In other words, to describe my perception as, on the one hand, a perception of Charles, or, on the other hand, a perception of his shape, is to ascribe a different object to each perception and thus, from the intentional point of view, to describe *different experiences*. From the intentional point of view, perceiving Charles's shape is not a part of perceiving Charles; it is another perception altogether. In fact, if I pay attention to his shape as such, I will probably perceive him differently.

Secondly, if we do accept the idea that seeing Charles entails seeing some phenomenal content—his shape—we should inquire into the grammar pertaining to this sub-perception. It appears that, from a grammatical point of view, this perception cannot be of a different kind than the perception as a whole. A contrast is supposed to be made between 'what really appears' and 'what is perceived as a whole, without necessarily appearing.' However, we should ask whether a shape as such—I am not even talking of *Charles's shape*—ever really 'appears' in the *absolute* sense that is required.

According to the story we have told, 'phenomenal content' is not merely a distinguishable part of the 'intentional content' of perception. As it is intentional it is also supposed to be an *object*. A shape, for example, is certainly an object. Yet does an object ever 'appear' in the sense required by this notion of phenomenal content? There are sensible, for example, visible, features of objects—Charles's shape, for example. It is not so obvious that Charles's philosophical talent is such a feature, though it makes good sense to say that, seeing him, I see a great philosopher.

Thus, from this perspective, we can distinguish two kinds of properties that belong to what we see: in seeing Charles, I see a philosopher, but—normally—I cannot see *that he is a philosopher*; however, I can see *that he has this shape.* Nonetheless, this distinction between sensible and non-sensible features of objects, or between sensible objects and non-sensible objects, is not a distinction between phenomenal and non-phenomenal objects or features of objects in the requisite sense. Since a sensible object is no less an object for being sensible, it logically follows that *it always transcends the way it is supposed to 'appear.'*

For example, what is it to perceive a certain shape, if it is not to perceive a shape I or someone else could see *again on another occasion?* By characterizing what I see this way ("not Charles, just a shape"), *nolens volens* I have already stepped into intentional space. This means that *what I claim to see already exists beyond an alleged 'pure appearance.'* If I ask 'what is really given to me in perception' it might seem a good response—call it the 'eye-doctor response'—to say: unstable colour patches that change from time to time. When I characterize them as constituting a certain *shape*, I assign an identity to them. This identity, as such, is not given: it is a *norm.* Now, does this mean we should retreat the whole distance from shapes and similar objects to colour patches and other kinds of fuzzy, momentary entities? Perhaps these are the real *phenomenal objects* of sight.

However, this retreat does not constitute a solution. To say that I cannot really see the shape, but only some momentary colour patches and flashes, raises exactly the same problem as before. Firstly, some quite specific circumstances are required for me to be able to say that. Secondly, if I really do say that, I treat those patches and flashes as *objects* of perception. Now, the grammar of objects is the grammar of identity. I can say that I have seen this colour patch only if it makes sense to recognize it on another occasion, or at least to suppose I can talk about the very same patch on another occasion. This 'identity,' however, is never 'given.' Or more precisely: it is never given in the sense required by those who think that 'phenomenal content'—as opposed to merely intentional content—is absolute. Of course, in the regular sense of 'given' according to which 'to be given' is to be given by a certain standard—and so, according to a norm—Charles is certainly 'given' to me in perception. As a matter of fact, there is no other way to be 'given.'

Thus, if we want 'phenomenal content' to be intentional, it must be one among many parts that together constitute perceptual content. Calling such content 'phenomenal' does not render it exceptional. Ultimately, in fact, it is unclear why we should call it 'phenomenal' at all. If by this we mean that such content only entails *sensible* features of the object, then we should observe that the border between what is sensible and what is intelligible in perception is not always sharply drawn. What should we say about *nice*, or *intelligent smiles?* Is there nothing to them that is sensible? Which aspects of them do I *really* see? In these cases, the distinction does not seem to apply. In fact, what is considered 'sensible' crucially depends on how many sensible marks the concepts we apply in perception already contain.

Anyway, why call the properties of sensible objects '*phenomenal,*' as if they belonged to another grammar? Are they not, logically speaking, properties like any others? As long as we treat phenomenal content as a particular kind of intentional content, it will be impossible to isolate it from what we would consider, in any given circumstance, the intentional content of a perception. 'Phenomenal content' is not a kingdom within the kingdom of perception, for one cannot stop halfway in the language game of intentionality.

It seems, however, that one possibility remains open: perhaps phenomenal content is not intentional content. I have no problem with this solution in principle, except for the fact that I cannot see clearly what such content could be. What could content that is *neither true nor false* be?

It seems to me that some friends of 'phenomenal content' understand it as being what I would call '*de facto* content.' In other words, there is, on the one hand, what my perception *represents* to me—that things are this or that way—something which can be true or false (we can leave open the question of whether we should still call it perception if it is false, or if so, what it is a perception of). On the other hand, there is what we feel in this perception—and that is something neither true nor false, but just is what it is. I call this '*de facto* content,' as it is nothing but the fact that I feel this or that way in a given perception.

Now, the first question to ask, if we accept this notion of 'phenomenal content,' is whether it is possible to talk of *the* phenomenal content of *a* perception. Perhaps it is possible to speak of one *perception*—if such a thing exists—because it is supposed to be a momentary episode, and therefore discrete. However, how do we individuate a single perception, except by its *object?* The problem is that, according to the new sense of 'phenomenal content' that we have just introduced, there is not a specific 'phenomenal content' for a single perception, but rather an infinity of possible 'phenomenal contents.' For if we completely separate the 'phenomenal content' of perception from its 'intentional content,' there is no reason to think that an individual perception might not be felt in infinitely many ways.

Of course, there is still the possibility that there is something specific *it feels like to perceive this or that.* In fact, this is certainly the case. It is what we call: *perceiving this or that.* From this point of view, the phenomenal and intentional contents are impossible to tell apart. Thus, we must identify the *phenomenal content* of a perception with its *intentional content*, or else it will be impossible to individuate the content. From this point of view, what we have called '*de facto* content' will not do. There is no '*de facto* content' of *a single perception.*

That said, the notion in question is entirely unclear. Admittedly, it is difficult to make sense of the idea of a perception that I do not 'feel' in any way. *There is something it is like* to taste a pineapple—it's like a lot of things, in fact. However, it is very strange to make a separate content out of these feelings—a 'phenomenal content.' The 'content'

I am presented with—if we want to talk this way—is the pineapple or perhaps the taste of the pineapple (depending on the circumstances, I would describe it in one of these two ways). The way I feel just is the way I am presented with what I am presented with, whatever that may be. Thus, *logically*, I cannot be presented with this feeling, not because it is hidden—because I need, for instance, some act of reflection to disclose it—but because *there is nothing to be disclosed*, except for the fact that *I am having a perceptual experience*. 'The way it feels to have it' does not constitute a separate content. In fact, it is not a content at all. Only those who conflate the two sides of the concept of experience—experience as *something I have* and experience as *of something*—could think otherwise. An experience is not an experience of itself or of any other 'experience.' That idea makes no sense. I do not experience experiences: I *have* them.

CHAPTER FIVE

The Radicality of Perception

Beyond Conjunctivism and Disjunctivism

THE DISPUTE between *conjunctivism* and *disjunctivism* has become a central issue in contemporary philosophy of perception. In the context of this dispute, *disjunctivism* seems, *prima facie,* a very attractive hypothesis. For if *conjunctivism* is a theory according to which there is some element shared by perceptual states and states that are not perceptual—a 'common factor'—it would appear to have undesirable consequences for the nature of *real, full-blooded perception.* Indeed, this conception seems to suggest that real perception depends upon the processing or interpretation of the so-called 'common element,' as if these states were first *something other than perceptual,* before becoming what they are: perceptions. Thus, one could say that conjunctivism is to some extent arguing against *the originality of perception*—the fact that perception provides us with something unique that cannot be gotten from elsewhere.

However, one must keep in mind that conjunctivism is to some extent what Austin would have called a 'trouser-word.'[1] I sincerely doubt that many people call themselves 'conjunctivists.' Of course, many philosophers endorse a 'common factor' theory of perception and similar states; disjunctivism historically developed as a critical reaction to this kind of theory. Nevertheless, it is clear that *'conjunctivism'* has come to function as a kind of straw man in the contemporary philosophical debate.

---

1. See Austin 1964, p. 70.

In fact, when we pay attention to the labels themselves, we find that they are not quite symmetric—they function differently from one another. By disjunctivism, we may mean the theory according to which, when we have an experience of a perceptual 'style' (I use this term in order to remain as neutral as possible) *either* it is a genuine perception (i.e., a perception of something in the world, whether an object or a fact), *or* it is a completely different sort of state. Consequently, our experience can be described using a *disjunction*. But we find no real counterpart to this idea in so-called 'conjunctivism.' Experience, for the latter, is in no way correctly described using a *conjunction*. It makes no sense to say that we have both a perception *and* a perceptual-style experience that is not a perception. Thus, conjunctivism, if there is such a thing, is not about conjunction—whereas disjunctivism really does involve a disjunction. The essence of conjunctivism resides in its affirmation of *a common element*, which does not itself amount to a conjunction. Thus, to talk of *conjunctivism*, is to some extent already to adopt the viewpoint of *disjunctivism*.

Like many philosophers today, I am fairly sympathetic to the disjunctivist perspective. I am *negatively* sympathetic to it insofar as I have misgivings about the way conjunctivism—if such a thing exists—must treat perception as something *non-original* since, for it, perception results from something being added to an element that is not, *per se*, perception. In other words, it treats perception as something essentially *analyzable*. This is what makes me so reluctant, for, in this matter, I consider perception to be the basis (not the *analysandum*) of the analysis.

However, on further inspection, I am not sure that disjunctivism is in a much better position. As a matter of fact, it seems to me to be more or less in the same boat, insofar as, like conjunctivism (at least the kind that disjunctivism targets under this label), disjunctivism is essentially an *epistemological view*. Now, there are many questions that can be raised regarding the relevance to perception of such kind of view. I would like to address two: Firstly, is disjunctivism really a view about perception *as such*? Secondly, if—as I suspect—it is not, and is instead an essentially *epistemological* view regarding the *knowledge* we can have on the basis of perception, is it at least satisfactory? Again, I suspect the answer is 'no.'

The analysis I am going to develop—one I hope is true to the Austinian tradition—will, paradoxically, vindicate the 'conjunctivist' hunch that there really is something that perceptions and *states that seem like perceptions* share, namely . . . that they are perceptions! Of course, this claim is pretty far from what is usually meant by 'conjunctivism' in the contemporary philosophical debate. However, consistently pursued, it is also incompatible with true 'disjunctivism'—a position that should, contrary to what one sometimes reads nowadays,[2] be the target of Austinian criticism just as much as 'conjunctivism' is.

To begin with we need to make a distinction. 'Disjunctivism,' as opposed to 'conjunctivism,' makes a quite general point. As we said, it consists in rejecting the idea that mental states that are genuine perceptions share with those that are not the same kind of mental substate as their basis. The question then is, what kinds of mental states might we be tempted to think of as sharing such a substate with perception?

It seems that two different kinds of answer are possible. Firstly, there is a merely philosophical or conceptual answer: it is enough to be a state that 'seems like perception,' but where some essential aspect of perception is missing. Usually the aspect in question is *the real relation to an object.* Thus, one constructs the philosophical concept of *'something that seems like perception, but which lacks what is proper to perception: having an object.'* If we really want to make a point about perception as such, the important question is whether *anything like this* in fact exists.

Secondly, we can consider the problem from an empirical standpoint, where two kinds of case are relevant. On the one hand, what is usually called 'illusion.' On the other hand, what is usually called 'hallucination.' Philosophers tend to treat these similarly when they

2. See for instance Soteriou 2009.

are addressing problems in the philosophy of perception on a purely speculative level. And perhaps we can do so if we are content—as philosophers usually are—with a merely conceptual determination of illusions and hallucinations. In that case the difference between them will be as follows: an illusion will be thought of as *a perceptual-style experience of a real object that is nevertheless not presented as it really is*; a hallucination will be *a perceptual-style experience in which no real object is presented.*

Now, if these perceptual-style experiences are considered from the point of view of their truth-value, the situation may seem to be the same in both cases. If an experience doesn't present things as they are, isn't it simply *false?* Leaving aside the issue of whether this makes sense with respect to *presenting* as opposed to *representing*— is presenting things otherwise than they are really *presenting* them?—one might nevertheless attempt a qualification here. An experience that presents things as being 'other than they are' is indeed false. However, if an experience presents things *that are not* (granting this is possible, at least in some sense), is it even *false?* We might be inclined to say that, at least in some cases, such an experience is below the level of truth and falsity, that it has no truth-value at all. For concerning what is not, something (i.e., an experience) can be neither true nor false.

However, on a 'fact-like' conception of the object of perceptual experience, one might reply that, even in the latter sort of situation, the object is still presented as *being some way:* that is to say, as *being.* After all, does not a strong impression and perhaps even conviction of reality belong to the phenomenology of what is ordinarily called 'hallucination'?

Either way the philosophical and merely *a priori* approach is often far too keen to conflate two cases which it might be worth distinguishing; especially if, as I believe, one should first of all *ask whether either of them actually exists.*

As a matter of fact, what is embarrassing about the conjunctivism / disjunctivism debate is that it seems to largely be a philosophical construct. As a rule, the case of the misleading non-perception that only seems to be a perception is too abstract to make any sense. It is a mere product of theory. Once we take a closer look at the phenomena in order to flesh out the problem phenomenologically, we can immediately see that it is necessary to distinguish the two different cases. But it is not clear that in either case there is anything that could make sense of the philosophical construct. We should therefore ask whether there are any real 'illusions' or real 'hallucinations' in the merely conceptual sense we defined. I am not going to answer the question in relation to hallucination, as it is a far more difficult case than illusion. I should like, however, to formulate some doubts about the traditional picture of the problem—that is, about 'hallucinations in the philosophical sense of the term.'

If, by 'hallucination,' we understand some state in which—if this expression makes sense—we are 'presented with an object that is not,' then there is probably something that corresponds to this phenomenologically. The pink elephant that someone suffering from *delirium tremens* sees, simply *is not*. It does not exist. Now, and this is the important point, in seeing it she has a strong sense of its reality; it has the kind of *presence* characteristic of perception as an experience (the canonical experience?) of reality.

However, should we be so certain that the state experienced in such a hallucination is that similar, phenomenologically, to ordinary perception? The mere fact that it is usually experienced as a *disturbance* is already evidence to the contrary. On the other hand, more fine-grained analyses of modified states of consciousness that have recently been developed[3] suggest that what allegedly makes hallucinations seem similar to real perceptions is in fact what *distinguishes* the former from the latter: genuine hallucinations are apparently characterized by an *overdeveloped* sense of reality that is not found in ordinary perception—and this very feature disqualifies hallucinations as a basis for knowledge. (In fact, it is rather uncommon for

3. See González 2004.

someone to be *epistemically* misled by a hallucination.) So, *phenomenally* speaking, it is difficult to assimilate hallucinations and perceptions—at least from the point of view of the respective cognitive role each state plays.

Now, there is another possible view of the states in question that leaves to one side the problem of their epistemic status and considers them 'in themselves,' as *experiences*. From this perspective, it is perhaps not impossible to put things the other way around, asserting that hallucinations are just *a particular kind of perception* (a kind it is difficult to define, as it intertwines elements pertaining to its *lack* of epistemic value as well as its specific phenomenology). Hallucination, on this analysis, will count as *a pathological case of perception*—but, as with anything pathological, it will still belong to the realm of what it is a pathology of—in this case perception.

What is the philosophical significance of the view that hallucination, although a very specific kind (a somehow *excessive* kind) of perceptual experience, is nevertheless a perceptual-style experience when considered phenomenologically? One might expect the upshot to be a *conjunctivist* approach to hallucination. However, nothing necessitates this. Is it so obvious that hallucinations are, in accordance with Jean-Étienne Esquirol's classical definition, 'perceptions without objects'? That, in the case of hallucination, our relation to real objects—which is characteristic of perception according to a certain naïve realism—is broken? Is a hallucination really ever a hallucination of *nothing*?

The question is complicated by the fact that we must not mistake the intentional point of view for the relational one. It is possible to maintain that every hallucination has an *intentional object* without supposing it has a *real object* and thus counts as perceptual according to naïve realism. If so, it is possible to develop a kind of disjunctivist perspective according to which, on the one hand, perception is *relational*, and, on the other hand, hallucination is a completely different kind of state that is essentially *intentional*, but not relational. Nevertheless, such a conception seems unrealistic given the phenomenological observation that the character of hallucinatory experience is markedly perceptual.

On the other hand, when maintaining that hallucination does not constitute a break with reality—as it might seem to from a perspective contaminated by epistemology—but in fact shares the very relation to reality that perception has, one must bear in mind that a *causal* relation is not sufficient. Of course, one would probably be perfectly justified in saying that no hallucination lacks a genuine cause. However, according to the naïve realist's relational theory of perception, what matters is not the reality of the cause of perceptual experience so much as *the reality of what is experienced in perception*—the fact that perception really is the experience of something, where that means 'something real.' Thus, the point is whether, and in what sense, that which is experienced in hallucination is 'real.'

However, perhaps a more relevant question is what, in hallucination, is *not* real? The answer, apparently, is *that which would be tempted to describe as 'the object of the experience' if we were to consider our experience as grounds for knowledge.* But should we consider it grounds for knowledge in those circumstances? On the other hand, we *genuinely experience* the hallucination, and—what is more difficult to make sense of philosophically—what we experience is accompanied by a strong sense of reality.

Now, I would like to suggest that what we hallucinate is a part of the reality we perceive. This is because no hallucination exists in isolation—at least not in absolute isolation: every perceptual hallucination[4] essentially occurs against a background of reality—as *part of a real perceptual scene.* Hallucination, as such, is always a kind of localized *outgrowth of perception*, as it were. However, this fact could mislead us into accepting a theory that describes every hallucination as *partial.* That is not quite the point. For, far from reducing the reality of the hallucinated content to what is given as its necessary background—the perceptual fabric on which it imposes its

4. I leave aside here the problem of dreams as it raises quite specific phenomenological issues.

motif, so to speak—we should probably instead say that *even what is hallucinated is real* and in precisely the way in which the basic reality of what perception in general presents us with is said to be real. *What is hallucinated is exactly what is seen—or, more often, heard.* As such, hallucination is a genuine part of the reality to which perception relates us—it is something that might happen *in* that reality. This specific notion of 'reality' certainly raises a lot of epistemological issues, for it is difficult to locate it in the framework we normally call 'reality'—as opposed to 'non-reality'—when adopting an epistemological point of view. Nonetheless, it refers, in some sense, to parts of reality we necessarily have dealings with—for what can the word 'reality' signify, at bottom, if not something 'we *have* to *deal with*'? More precisely: hallucinations are a part of what we see and hear (and so on), in the very sense in which we see and hear 'reality'—in fact that is exactly what we normally *mean* by 'hallucination.'

Paradoxically, this idea does not entail the conjunctivist claim that there must be something common to both perception and non-perceptual experience (in this case, hallucination). On the contrary, according to this view hallucination *just is perception*—but it is a form of perception that makes it hard to comprehend the idea, true in general, that perception affords us *reality*. For it is difficult to make sense of the latter concept separately from its *epistemological* meaning.

In order to investigate further the claim that even those perceptual experiences (the important word being 'perceptual') that we are tempted to think of as failing to present things as they are, *do* in fact confront us with reality, we should return to the case of illusion. This is because, philosophically speaking, the account I have suggested treats hallucinations as *extreme cases* of illusion, despite the fact that it allows for significant phenomenological and empirical differences between hallucination and illusion. This suggestion is different from the one I criticized above, in which illusion is just treated as a kind of hallucination. (Representing things as other than they are—in the case of a so-called perceptual experience—would then consist in representing *nothing* and therefore would not be representation at all.) On the contrary: the suggestion is that hallucinations are only borderline cases of perception—while so-called 'illusions' are *perceptions pure and simple*, although they might be thought to have quite particular cognitive consequences of their own. Therefore, I will make my point clearer by focusing on illusions in the sense previously advanced, as well as the corresponding sense of *reality*.

Illusions are a common occurrence that clearly belong to the sphere of perceptual experience. Now, if by 'illusion' we mean the experience of something *real* where the thing experienced in fact differs from how we are irresistibly tempted to describe it, then illusion resists the sort of characterization a radical disjunctivist will be inclined to make of it. For, exactly like perception (in the canonical sense of the term), and in exactly the same way, *it is relational*. It exhibits, essentially, *the same kind of relation* to an object as perception does.

However, they still differ in an epistemologically crucial way: in one case the things the subject is related to are exactly as they are presented to her as being; in the other, it seems they are not. Now, it seems to me that this difference is illusory and that illusions, in some sense, just are perceptions (or are at least real parts of the perceptual landscape[5]). As a consequence they confront us with reality as such. Though not, perhaps, 'reality as it really is'—though from which perspective can this be said?

In order to make my point, I shall make use of Maurice Merleau-Ponty's wonderful analysis of a classic case of optical illusion in the *Phenomenology of Perception*. Although I do not completely agree

---

5. Once more: the point is not to deny the phenomenological peculiarity of 'illusions' (or at least of some of the experiences called illusions), only their *philosophical* peculiarity relative to perceptions.

with it, he nevertheless has a brilliant hunch which is relevant to the evaluation of both conjunctivism and disjunctivism.

What is the traditional account of the Müller-Lyer illusion? Although both lines are the same size, we see the line whose arrows are facing *inwards* as being shorter than the other line. Usually we only have to look at two lines in order to know whether one is shorter than the other. This is what we would call *seeing something as shorter*. However, what is particular to the Müller-Lyer experience is that although we see one line as being shorter than the other it turns out that in fact it is not—something we can verify via a simple geometrical construction (namely, the perpendicular projection of one line segment onto the other). As such it appears that in this case *we cannot see things as they really are*.

This, at any rate, is the phenomenology of the Müller-Lyer experience according to the traditional conception, contaminated as it is by the endemic conjunctivism of modern psychology and philosophy of perception. It presupposes that, in some cases, what we see is a correct representation of a situation, in other cases, a false one. Yet in both cases the representation is of the same kind, it is just that in one case we see one of the lines as being shorter than the other. Conversely, disjunctivism seems committed to saying that in one case we have a full-blooded experience of seeing—one that presents us with the situation *as it really is*—and that in the other case we have an experience that *seems like a perception of the situation* but that in fact does not relate us to its *reality*. As such it is simply a different kind of experience.

However, solely from the perspective of an analysis of perception, it is difficult to maintain that basic 'optical illusions' fail to be genuine cases of perception. Isn't that just the *way we see lines* when they're fitted with inverse arrows? If so, isn't perception misleading? Is it not the case that *we see the things other than they are?* It is possible, at least in some contexts, to answer the first question in the affirmative. It is more difficult to do so with the latter, as the question then is: *What do we really see?* And, after all, it is not at all certain that our first answer—that 'one line is shorter than the other'—makes proper sense in the way we intended it.

Sometimes perception can be misleading because we, being the way we are, are tempted to describe what is given in perception in a way that does not match up with how things *really* are. However, does this therefore mean that we actually *see* things as being a way they are *not?* It is here that Merleau-Ponty proves so helpful. In a beautiful phenomenological analysis of the case, he says:

> The two straight lines in Müller-Lyer's optical illusion are neither of equal nor unequal length; it is only in the objective world that this question arises.[6]

This analysis has the merit (although, as we shall see, its background is still questionable) of reminding us that there is no equality or inequality except through a *standard* we apply to the situation, and that when we investigate whether what is given to us in perception conforms to this standard or not, we need first to have asked what it is we are after and whether the standard is relevant or not.

From one point of view—that which Merleau-Ponty calls 'the objective world'—a certain standard is indeed relevant. It is possible to measure both lines and establish that they are 'equal.' One can even give some visual evidence for this by superimposing one segment on the other, or by linking the ends of both segments. On the other hand, it is difficult 'to see that' without any additional construction. *Prima facie,* the segments do not look 'the same size.' But do they look as though they are definitely *different* sizes? It is not clear that they do. In an ordinary situation, were we not forced to say 'yes' or 'no,' it is likely that we would hesitate to say for certain one way or another—despite being tempted to say that they are different. The only thing that would be clear to us is that the lines 'look different.'

Merleau-Ponty's brilliant move is simply to draw our attention to this point: if the segments *look* different, it is obvious that they *are*

6. Merleau-Ponty 1958, p. 6.

different. Indeed, a line with arrows facing *in* is not the same thing as a line with arrows facing *out*. So it makes perfect sense that, when presented together, our perception of them is contrasted. By adding arrows to a line we obviously alter it. Thus, seeing the unadorned line and seeing the line with arrow-like ends is not the same thing— and whether the arrows are facing 'in' or 'out' also makes a difference. Isn't it logical, therefore, that the line looks different in each case? 'A segment with the arrows facing 'in' looks like that; and a segment with the arrows facing 'out' looks like this.' In other words: 'this is *what it is to see a segment with the arrows facing 'in'*; this is *what it is to see 'the same' segment with the facing arrows out'* (in fact it is a *different figure*[7]).

However, doesn't this entail that we see 'the same' line as having different sizes, that is to say, as being unequal to itself? Merleau-Ponty queries this:

> In Müller Lyer's illusion, one of the lines ceases to be equal to the other without becoming 'unequal': it becomes 'different.'[8]

The problem, therefore, does not concern what we see: we really *do* see different things. The problem concerns the judgment we make to the effect that what we see are two 'unequal' lines. But, in fact, *this is not what we see:* we simply see two lines in different contexts; we see *different sensible Gestalts*. Now, what does it mean to say that we cannot see that the lines 'are unequal'? Merleau-Ponty's explanation of why this is impossible causes difficulties. He maintains that "we must recognize the indeterminate as a positive phenomenon,"[9] by which he means to affirm that what we perceive is positively indeterminate (by the standard, that is, of so-called 'objective thought').

---

7. And "an isolated, objective line, and the same line taken in a figure, ceases to be, for perception, the same" (Merleau-Ponty 1958, p. 13). See also the Gestaltic analysis of Zöllner's optical illusion (Merleau-Ponty 1958, p. 41).
8. Merleau-Ponty 1958, p. 13.
9. Merleau-Ponty 1958, p. 7.

Personally, I am unsure whether this kind of assertion makes sense. I would like to say that what we see is, in itself, neither determinate nor indeterminate. *It just is what it is.* Certainly, it is not determinate so long as we do not apply a standard to it. Nevertheless, as long as the standard is relevant in the circumstances then by applying it we will usually obtain a result as determinate as can be expected given the particular standard we bring to bear. For example, if we measure both lines we shall find they are equal. Insofar as it makes sense to apply a standard of equality to them—and it certainly does, contrary to what Merleau-Ponty seems somehow to suggest—their status is perfectly determinate.

What is missing then? In this case, it seems to be that what is perceptually given does not *suggest* equality. Indeed, the lines really do look different. The reality of a perceptual difference which it is impossible to make sense of by appeal to *some* standard we would be inclined to apply to this perception is the characteristic feature of 'perceptual illusions.' The problem is that we cannot find any trace of the determination we are looking for in the perceptual appearance. If asked, we would probably feel uneasy and hesitate before saying that the lines are 'unequal.' We feel that there is something peculiar about the figure. However, without being familiar with the illusion, we would probably not be able to say that the lines 'are equal'; and we cannot claim to see that they are, even if this is exactly what it is to see two lines of the same size, one ending with arrows facing in and the other with arrows facing out.

Now, the apparent impossibility of basing 'the correct knowledge' (insofar as what we want to know is whether both lines are 'equal' or not) on our perception says less about our perception and more about the conceptual framework we attempt to apply to it. Our perception is really just perception of what there is. Once more, this is precisely what it is to see lines of the same size, one of them ending with arrows facing inwards and the other with arrows facing outwards. In itself there is no 'illusion' here, only full contact with reality in all its peculiarity. However, there seems to be a gap between the perceptual presence of these things and the concepts we try to apply to them: the equality of the lines is not recognizable in the perceptual experience (at least not without altering them). Of course, we can trace the parallels linking the ends of both lines, such that it will be manifest that these lines are the same size—we would then say that we can 'see' as much. However, we should apply what Merleau-Ponty says about 'attentive,' 'analytic' perception to this sort of alteration: "instead of revealing the 'normal sensation,' [it] substitute[s] a special set-up for the original phenomenon."[10]

The question then is, why do we find the Muller-Lyer illusion so surprising that we talk of a 'perceptual illusion,' where we find only *a particular kind of perception.*

The answer does not lie in the nature of this particular kind of perception, but rather in the nature of the conceptual apparatus through which we view it. For the very concepts we use in such cases (e.g., 'size' or 'equality') *usually do bear some connection to perception.* Or, more precisely, they are *rooted in perception:* they are partially dependent on it. Of course, there are uses of the concepts of size and equality that are not perceptual and so not dependent on perception. Nonetheless, for instance, the notion of estimating a length *intuitively* makes sense. Moreover, it seems clear that intuitive estimation plays a genealogical role in setting up our concepts of size and equality, or at least some such concepts—a *paradigmatic* role. Of course, there may be other relevant concepts that do not depend to the same extent on perception, and that can do without a perceptual paradigm. However, it does not seem absurd to think that, in our natural picture of the world, these concepts, that is, *concepts that have made perception itself a norm,* do play a central role.

Thus, the notion of 'perceptual illusion,' which suggests an 'error' found *in* perception, in fact registers a gap between the specific way in which we are presented with things in a given perception and the

10. Merleau-Ponty 1958, p. 9.

general perceptual determination that imbues some of our concepts. These concepts have made *some* aspects of our perception the norm, but not *all* of them—obviously not ones that are too particular, or that are generally unfit for acting upon. We call those features of perception that are left outside the system of our *perceptual concepts* (that is to say: concepts that, in their constitution, take up some perceptual features) 'perceptual illusions.' A proof of this point is that there are many features of perception that are in fact not much different from what we call 'perceptual illusions,' but which it would never occur to us to describe as such. Because they belong to the regular fabric of our perception, we consider them 'normal.' We have made them part of our conceptual framework insofar as that framework is constitutively linked to what is perceived as such— the perceived *insofar* as it is perceived. The question is not whether in itself our perception conforms to a norm that defines what there can be (as opposed to what cannot be), but rather how much of the perceived we have incorporated into our definition of that norm.

I am inclined to say that an outcome of this inquiry into the epistemological significance of so-called 'perceptual illusions'[11]—one that has followed in the footsteps of Austin and Travis[12]—is that the point made by disjunctivism is an *imaginary* one. Certainly, on my account, conjunctivism is wrong in holding that, in addition to (and in front of) perceptions, there are states that share something with them although they are not perceptions themselves. For those states that are the natural candidates for playing such a role, that is, *illusions*, just *are* perceptions on my account. However, if they are perceptions, we do not need to say that 'either we have a perception *or*

11. Of course, there is a lot more to be said about them. The concept of 'perceptual illusion' I have been concerned with and that belongs to the position I have criticized (which is essentially an epistemological position) is highly general and abstract. Psychologically and phenomenologically, distinctions should be made that cannot be without broaching a real philosophy of perception—that is to say, a philosophy concerned with *the reality of perception*.

12. See Austin 1964; see Travis 2004.

something else'; we simply *have a perception* in every case where we may be inclined to say that we do.

This claim is possibly excessive, at least in relation to hallucinations. In their case further distinctions rooted in the particular complexity of the concept of hallucination would need to be made. (It is very difficult to say what is *perceptual* and what is not, when dealing with such a murky concept.) At any rate this analysis, at least when applied to illusions, seems to deflate the importance of disjunctivism.

The upshot seems clear: *disjunctivism is not, as such, a position in the philosophy of perception.* As a matter of fact it is not at all concerned with the individual reality of perception, and is even less interested in defending the *originality* of perception. It is merely an epistemological point concerning the role perception can play in knowledge that we claim to have of the world.

Now, I think that disjunctivism is highly questionable, even when considered as a merely *epistemological* position. I am not going to elaborate on this here (to some extent I have already indirectly addressed it in Chapter 2) but I can briefly say this much: If I go to the washroom, there is little chance (though not *no* chance) that the Christmas tree in the living room will burst into flames before I return. Should I say for all that that 'either everything will be fine when I come back or the Christmas tree will be on fire'? It seems to me there is not much point to the 'either-or' here. Certainly, in an *absolute* sense, it is true. But the question is whether the disjunction *makes sense*. It certainly will if there is, objectively, some *particular reason* to think that something might happen to the tree. However, in the absence of such a reason, it makes no sense.

Of course, we might make all of our factual assertions take this form, that is, make them all *disjunctions*. However, this approach more or less amounts to the one Austin mocks in this famous passage:

> If you are aware you may be mistaken, you oughtn't to say you know, just as, if you are aware you may break your word, you have no

business to promise. But of course, being aware that you may be mistaken doesn't mean merely being aware that you are a fallible human being: it means that you have some concrete reason to suppose that you may be mistaken in this case. Just as "but I may fail" doesn't mean merely "but I am a weak human being" (in which case it would be no more exciting than adding "D.V."): it means that there is some concrete reason for me to suppose that I shall break my word. It is naturally always possible ("humanly" possible) that I may be mistaken or may break my word, but that by itself is no bar against using the expressions "I know" and "I promise" as we do in fact use them.[13]

It seems to me that we can apply these precise words to the so-called problem of perceptual illusion as well. To be sure, it sometimes happens that we are misled by that which we call the *perceptually given* (though perhaps in calling it this we are already making a mistake), insofar as its similarity to the way things appear in other situations induces us to think that this situation is otherwise than it is. This even occurs in the midst of action—as when, for example, I walk toward the end of Borromini's gallery in the Palazzo Spada in Rome and it turns out to be much closer than I first took it to be. However, such situations are not nearly so common as certain philosophers would like them to be. Furthermore, the relative rarity of such cases—if not of perceptual illusion then at least of its disturbing cognitive effects—is good reason for us to take things at face value, as being 'exactly as they seem.' That is as being, in other words, exactly the way the concepts we are naturally inclined to apply to them characterize them as being—*unless we have a particular reason to think otherwise.* Of course, I would not say the same things in a hall of mirrors. But neither would you. There are, certainly, situations in which it is very difficult to make sense of what one sees.

Thus, except in very specific situations (e.g., after contemplating the ceiling of the Sant'Ignazio church in Rome for too long) I cannot

13. Austin 1961, p. 98.

see the point of disjunctivism. The disjunctive formulation of perceptual knowledge seems to underestimate the incredible strength of perceptual evidence, a strength which stems from the fact that so many of our concepts are meant *for* perception, for *making something of it that we can call evidence.*

In other words, what doesn't seem to work in disjunctivism, from the cognitive point of view, is its *minimalism.* No doubt, disjunctivism is a 'modest' position.[14] *But is modesty in order when dealing with perception?* Perceptual knowledge (that is, knowledge directly based on perception) seems far more *committed* than that.

There are two ways to negate a disjunction. The first consists in negating its constituent parts and then affirming the conjunction of their negation. This is, to some extent, what conjunctivism does. For if conjunctivism is correct it turns out that the characterizations of real and illusory perception proposed by disjunctivism (at least on a canonical version of it)—that is, a direct relation to the perceived and something that has nothing substantial in common with perception—both turn out to be *false.* However, there is a second way: in ordinary language one can correct a disjunction by insisting that *there is no point in saying* "either *p* or *q*," because, in fact, it is just the case to say *p.*

I think the best response to disjunctivism, *in general,* is the latter.

14. See Martin 2004.

CHAPTER SIX

(Perceptual) Things Being What They Are

In his 1994 book, *Mind and World*, John McDowell makes a claim that has proven to be highly controversial: the content of perception is conceptual.

In claiming this his intent is perfectly clear. Against a naturalistic picture of the world, according to which perception is a merely (first-)natural occurrence, McDowell wants to return perception to the significant role it plays in our lives. Perception matters to what we think (as well as what we do) about the world insofar as it is a way for things to be *given* to us. However, to be given is to be given according to a norm—as satisfying or failing to satisfy this or that norm. And there are no norms except conceptual ones.

I think that at this level of analysis Charles Travis and John McDowell are in agreement. For, if, according to Travis's view, perception is not intentional—yet it remains essential to perception that one can make *intentional use of it*. It is essential that I can be said to see something in accordance with a theoretical framework or expectation. In this sense there is a *logical space of perception*. My perception is *what, depending on the circumstances, can be described in various ways*. This is essential to the logic of perception.

It is not so easy, thus, to identify where the real divergence between Travis and McDowell lies. Travis certainly doesn't endorse reductive naturalism's view of perception. What he is interested in is perception's importance in our human, therefore rational, life and thought. Nonetheless, McDowell himself indicated very clearly what the point of controversy is. McDowell's view is not only that concepts are eminently *applicable* to perception, but that they are *always already* applied to it—this formulation highlights the connection, explicit in *Mind and World*, to hermeneutics, in which it is very familiar. A trace of the 'Myth of the Given' always remains if one fails to conceive the content of perception as conceptual, something that, according to McDowell, Travis fails to do.

McDowell's description of Travis's position is certainly correct. However, the consequences he draws from this—and which he thinks tell against the position—are certainly mistaken. In order to see why, I am going to focus on McDowell's 'reply' to Travis's 'Reason's Reach,'[1] for it seems to me that this text gets to the bottom of things.

At the basis of Travis's rejection of McDowell's conceptualism is the need to make sense of *the facticity of perception*. Travis's basic intuition—which he shares with the other members of the *Oxonian realist* tradition that he belongs to—is not so much that in perception 'things are *given* as they are' (a claim which, had he endorsed it, would indeed make him prey to the 'Myth of the Given'), but that in perception, 'things are definitely as they are.'

If I see a piece of red meat on the rug then that's definitely how it is—redness and all. It is a chunk of reality. Some philosophers would say that my perception grants me 'access' to this chunk of reality. As if there were *the perceived meat* playing the part of an intermediary between my consciousness and the real piece of meat lying on the rug. Although common, this view is mistaken: it is part of our ordinary concept of perception that *the perceived meat* just is *the real meat*. Of course, sometimes we say that *we cannot perceive things as they really are* and the philosophy of perception owes us a story about such cases. As a matter of fact, this is an important aspect of the debate between Travis and McDowell. Even so, we should probably admit that it is *the meat itself* that we cannot perceive correctly. We still perceive the real meat—what else would we perceive?—it is

1. In Lindgaard 2008, pp. 258–267.

just that in certain circumstances we cannot perceive it as it really is, and thus our *genuine* perception of it, in all its *reality*, does not satisfy us epistemically.

At any rate, the idea is that perception is fundamentally an experience in which we are *presented with a piece of reality*—as opposed to a mental episode in which we *represent* something as being real.

One should observe that, to some extent, the converse is true. As true as it is that the concept of reality is in some sense part of the ordinary concept of perception, it is just as true that the concept of perception is part of our concept of reality, insofar as the perceived is, as such, a substantial part of what we call 'reality.' In the somewhat peculiar philosophical debates concerning the reality of the perceived or the capacity of perception to 'access' reality, one should always start by asking what is meant by 'reality.' In fact, the concept of *the perceived* constitutes a very important standard for what counts as 'reality,' as well as an important part of what is called 'reality.'

Now, if the perceived falls on the side of reality, this means that *it is what it is*—which is just what I call 'the facticity of perception.' The meat that I perceive on the rug at a certain point is exactly as it is. I cannot do anything to change this. Of course, I can take another look at it. However, that is just another perception, and as such another chunk of reality: a new piece-of-meat-on-the-rug-at-a-definite-time, just as real as the previous one. One can imagine my successive glances as a series of snapshots—as so many glimpses of reality.

An argument in support of the facticity of perception is the fact that it is essentially unrevisable, a feature which surfaces in what are traditionally labelled—perhaps wrongly—'perceptual illusions.' I may *know* that the stick in the water is not broken, but *I still see it as I see it*—'as if it were broken,' as philosophers traditionally have said—or, more correctly, as an unbroken stick submerged in water. So-called perceptual illusions are perceptions just like any other.

They belong to the reality of perception and, as such, to reality *simpliciter*. The stick's appearance when submerged in water is in some sense part of the reality of the stick: a stick is a thing that, when plunged into water, looks that way. This aspect of the stick is no more unnatural or unreal than how it appears outside of water in broad daylight. When we deal with a piece of reality as something that can be perceived, we deal with it as something that can take on certain appearances in certain circumstances.

In the philosophy of perception we commonly encounter the strange idea that there are perceptions that are, so to speak, by their nature true and those that are, by their nature, false. In one case I see the stick as it is, in another not. However, this misses the fact that 'looking broken' in water is just part of what this kind of sensible object—that is, an object to be perceived—is. As such, the 'illusion' is an aspect of its *reality*.

I had an interesting experience, demonstrating just this point, when I visited an Anish Kapoor exhibition in Berlin with Sandra. This exhibition displayed, among other things, some early works in which the artist played with what we might call the reality of 'trompe-l'œil.' Sandra drew my attention to the fact that the majority of the works consisted in creating *the illusion of a 'trompe l'œil.'* That is to say they were exactly as they seemed, *prima facie*, to be. There were no actual 'trompe l'œil,' yet by the clever design of the artist there *seemed to be*.

Now *if a trompe l'œil is something you can fake, that means it is real*. It constitutes a real way for things to be. Talk of *the reality of perception*—or of perception as just a face (the face?) of reality—makes sense at precisely this level.

Now, if the perceived falls on the side of reality, this means that the perceived is not just *this* or *that*—something falling under this or that concept—but that it is *exactly what it is*. Everything real, is something—many things, in fact. However, these 'many things'—for example, a lost dinner, as well as proof of Sid's carelessness—are exactly what they are, no matter how I consider them, or what judgment I make of them. I can think and say a lot of things about them that are either true or false, but they remain what they are. That is what we call 'reality.'

If we want to make sense of perception as an experience in which we face some portion of reality ('as it is'), it is pivotal that we do not mistake the notion of something 'being what it is' for some particular *way to be.* Between these two notions lies the famous 'Fregean line' upon which Travis rightly places so much emphasis.

On one side of the line lies what simply *is:* for instance, this piece of bloody meat on the rug. As with everything real, it is exactly what it is. On the other side there are the many ways we might take that thing to be. For instance, we might characterize it as 'a coloured spot of bloody meat on the rug' ('the red touch that was missing in my Kapoor-esque artistic arrangement' would be another way of characterizing it). Between these sides of the line lies a gulf. Indeed, we must call it a *category difference.*

Anyway, the red meat, as it is visible on the rug, is what it is— but we can characterize it in many different ways. Now, *to say that it is what it is, is not to characterize it in any way.* However, before we adequately characterize it as being this or that, what we perceive is just what it is. But is this not—*horresco referens*—to once again relapse into the Myth of the Given?

I could adopt the line of argument here that claims that the perceived is precisely what is not *given* insofar as it does not fall under a concept, but just *is* (what it is). However this is in danger of sounding too sophisticated simply *because it sounds too simple* to the ear of the Neo-Kantian, who precisely makes a point of not accepting things as they are. In fact, there might be a significantly misguided metaphysical idea lurking behind the assertion that the perceived, in itself, is just what it is—and is therefore not conceptual. McDowell, at least, thinks so.

Indeed, this problem surfaces in his reply to Travis in the Lindgaard volume. McDowell has misgivings about the idea of perceived things being what they are. He assumes that Travis uses this phrase to refer to a guise under which things are *given* prior to being conceptualized. It's as though there were, on the one hand, things *being what they are* and, on the other, *their being this or that,* such that everything has two sides: the side that is perceived and the side that is conceptualized.

What McDowell misses in Travis's position is that the difference between something's *being what it is* and something's *being this or that* is a *category difference*. That is to say it is a *logical* difference, not a real one. Of course, for something to be what it is just is for it to be *this* and *that*. For the red meat on the rug to be what it is is for it to be red, on the rug, probably quite disgusting and many other things besides. It's nothing *else* than those things—but at the same time neither is it, logically speaking, the same as them. Precisely because, although it might be those things, it *could* be others.

Thus there is no *real* gulf between something's being what it is and its being this or that. Its being what it is is adequately captured by whatever we take it to be (when we're correct, that is). However, there remains a category difference—indeed, a *category gulf*: something's being what it is is no *particular* way for it to be. Contrary to what McDowell holds it is not even the *general form* that ways of being take. It is mere being—what people call 'reality.' Speaking in the way mathematicians do about 'the power of the continuum,' we can say that the perceived has *the power of reality*—not *the power of the represented*. It is what it is, and, because it is what it is, it can be called *this* or *that*. It is *true* that it is this or that—but what it *really* is is not true: it is *real*.

McDowell's objection would be sound if the perceived thing's being what it is were a *way of being something* additional to its being this or that. In that case the being would be 'given' by perception prior to, and independently of, any conceptualization. However, its being is nothing *more* than its being this or that: it is *what is adequately characterized as being this or that* when we describe what is perceived truly. The difference is not between one being and another, but between a being and *a take on it.* The perceived thing is not *given* independently of any conceptualization. It *is* independently of any conceptualization (it is just what it is). And conceptualization, when it succeeds, captures something 'being what it is' independently of any conceptualization. Otherwise conceptualization would be no conceptualization.

McDowell criticizes Travis for placing something beyond reason's reach, for he takes Travis to hold that the perceived thing, since it is not conceptualized, must therefore lie beyond every conceptualization. However, this is not the case. The fact that the perceived thing is not conceptualized *per se* in no way entails that it is beyond conceptualization. When we conceptualize what we see, our concepts simply apply to that piece of visible reality that we encounter in perception. The fact that we conceptualize it makes it no less real, and, categorically, does not change anything as to its visible reality. However, if successful, this conceptualization adequately captures the piece of visible reality in question.

Thus, reason, if it is full-blooded, reaches reality itself, including *perceived reality.* From this perspective it might seem that Travis and McDowell agree after all. Both share a realistic concept of reason. This means that, among other things, both hold that the perceived does not lie outside the space of reasons. As such, their divergence may ultimately prove scholastic.

However, behind these scholastic subtleties there may lie a substantive difference. McDowell makes a point of insisting that there remains a difference—even a gulf—between Travis's position and his own. He holds that even if, on Travis's view, reason does reach reality, it is impossible to understand how it can (at least without reverting to the Myth of the Given). For if reality is to be graspable by our thought, it must, he thinks, already be conceptualized. McDowell's idea, then, is that 'naked perception' is not conceptualizable. Fortunately it is never 'naked.' It is *always already conceptualized.* Thus, we arrive back at the hermeneutical formulation.

I think this picture involves a crude category mistake. For, once again, it entails that the simple being of the perceived is some other being than that which perception puts us in a position to describe as being *this* or *that*—as if it were a being *of the same kind*, but still *another being*. As if this simple being needed something in order to *become* something that might be adequately captured by a concept. This point, with its clearly transcendental flavour, is precisely what Travis has in view when he criticizes McDowell's position as leaving the being of the perceived *outside* reason's reach.

This criticism may sound paradoxical given that McDowell advocates *the unboundedness of the conceptual.* For on his view nothing lies outside the reach of the conceptual, and thus nothing lies outside the reach of reason—but *at what cost?*

To some extent McDowell's position recalls Wittgenstein's target when he is elucidating the grammar of expectation in the *Philosophical Grammar.*[2] Among other things Wittgenstein observes that something fulfils an expectation *not inasmuch as it is expected but inasmuch as it is what it is.* My expectation sets a standard, and what happens must be assessed according to it. In order for it to be assessed, nothing is required except my expectation—but what is expected is assessed just as it is. There is no point in saying that it must first be qualified as an expectable thing—by who knows what procedure—before it can be assessed by the standards of my expectation. For rendering it a possible object of expectation (or something 'unexpected,' i.e., a *negative* object of expectation) is precisely what my expectation does. Of course, the fact that it is expected or unexpected is not a fact about the happening, but a fact about *me.* All the happening does in this story is happen, that is, be exactly what it is. Of course, the fact that it fulfils the standard set by my expectation tells us something about what it is: the standard provides a good *measure* of the happening.

In other words, we do not need *first* to expect something, in order that it might be expected; we simply expect something—that is enough. In the same way, we do not need *first* to make things conceptualizable in order that we might conceptualize them. We just conceptualize

2. Wittgenstein 1974.

them. And what we conceptualize are the things themselves—which are what they are, and are not 'conceptualized things.'

As a matter of fact, McDowell's analysis of perceptual content appears to be marked by a kind of *redundancy*. As such it is toxic from a Wittgensteinian point of view, for everything that is not necessary is, in philosophy, harmful. It is as if things needed to be conceptualized in order for them to be conceptualized. We should respond by saying: yes, that is just what 'conceptualize' means. Why should you say it twice? *Either* a concept reaches reality—which is just what it is, and not merely 'reality insofar as it is conceptualized'—*or* it is not a concept, and is worth nothing. The phrase: 'reality insofar as it is conceptualized' embodies a grammatical mistake. Reality is reality, nothing else. And that is exactly what concepts are concerned with. It is a part of what concepts are that they apply to reality as it is independently of them. As such, under favourable circumstances (i.e., cases of 'positive fulfilment'), they are able to reach it. If they are genuine concepts, and are used correctly, they always reach it in some way, either positively or negatively.

Why should reality, in order to be conceptualizable, be placed on the *conceptual* side of the Fregean line that separates concepts from the nonconceptual things to which they are applied? Put like that, McDowell's story sounds incredible.

Now, all this raises the obvious question: How could a philosopher of McDowell's calibre claim that the perceived is conceptual if, as we've seen, this is sheer (categorical) nonsense? In fact, McDowell's claim only makes sense on the assumption that he thinks that the perceived is not a part of *reality*. I think this is the heart of the matter. It is what lies behind McDowell's reluctance to concede that perception is not representational.

This means that according to McDowell's view, the fact that, for example, the stick 'looks broken' in the water, is not part of the stick's being but is only part of *our perceptual experience of it*— which, apparently, represents it to us incorrectly.

McDowell's disjunctivism may lead him to say that the experience is not perceptual if it does not represent the stick correctly—that it is another kind of experience that is only apparently perceptual. However, it seems difficult to claim this in the case of so-called 'perceptual illusions' (cases of hallucination, in the philosophers' sense, if any such thing exists, are another matter). As we have previously seen, what we call ordinarily 'perceptual illusions' seem to be perceptual experiences like any others—it is just that they are ones that, in particular circumstances, turn out to be misleading, or are at odds with a given standard we are used to applying to what is perceived. As if *a specific thing were supposed to look a certain way, and no other.* Now, as a matter of fact, if we retain one and one point only from Travis's masterpiece of analysis, 'The Silence of the Senses,'[3] it should be that, however they look, *things always look exactly as they are.*

However, the reason for this is that *the way things look is just a part of what they are.* The face of something encountered in a given perception is an aspect of its reality. Under the kind of sodium lamplights found in the tunnel across the street Sandra's car does not *look* bronze. It *is* bronze.

Why does McDowell resist this idea, one that lies at the heart of Travis's perceptual realism? It is because he distinguishes between the thing's being and the fact that we perceive it. This seems reasonable, for if perception really possesses the reach that we have ascribed to it, it would appear to be characterized by its capacity to present us with the thing itself, that is to say with something that may not have been perceived. If perceived things really were just *perceived* things we would once again end up with a vicious redundancy.

Now, things that are perceived belong to a particular kind: they are *sensible things.* As such, they have sensible features that, so to speak, constitute the material of perception. These sensible features are just part of the reality of perceived things, insofar as they are sensible things. In certain circumstances, things look this way or

3. Travis 2004.

that. There is no choice in this matter—neither interpretation nor correction can change anything about the way they look. Of course, to some of us—for instance colour-blind people—things might look slightly different, but we are aware of this possibility and have made it part of our concept of sensible reality.

Now, is sensible reality a *special kind of reality* that is separate from what we generally call 'reality'? Is it as though, on the one hand, the stick in the water were broken in sensible reality and, on the other, unbroken in reality *simpliciter?* One should of course first of all reply by saying that the stick is *not* broken in sensible reality, but merely 'looks broken,' which is not the same at all. And through its particular way of 'looking broken' it looks exactly like what it is: that is to say, an unbroken stick standing in water.

Furthermore, with this clarification in place, it is possible to see that 'sensible reality' is nothing but *a part of reality itself.* Not everything in reality is sensible, and so perceivable. However, a good part of it is, and when it is perceived it is perceived *qua* reality.

Now, why should the sensible features of things, in all their circumstantial variability—for there is no perception that is not circumstantial, which, of course, is not the same as being 'contextual'—not be taken to be a part of reality, a part of what the sensible things we deal with in perception *are?* Because of some standard—that of modern objectivism—which presumes the reality of things to lie beyond all such appearances? However, whoever says as much is making use of a very particular standard of reality, one according to which, for example, only the so-called causal efficacy of reality matters. From this perspective, a red hammer will work as well as a green one. But what about a traffic light?

Of course, one can resist this denial of so-called phenomenal qualities by making some of them—ones that obtain in certain circumstances—part of the reality of the thing instead of transitory aspects of it. One might be reminded here of Wilfrid Sellars's story of the necktie salesman: in daylight you see the tie's real colour.

From this point of view it is perfectly legitimate to dismiss 'perceptual illusions' as not part of the *reality* of things. However, this is not a claim about perception. It depends on a particular norm that is applied to perception—a norm that defines which kind of 'reality' one is after. For all that, the look of something in a perceptual illusion is no less 'real'—no less part of its 'reality' in a broader sense of the term. It is what we are presented with, and deal with, as it really is. Is this not the fundamental sense of 'reality'? If the red colour of Sandra's car is real, its bronze colour in the tunnel is no less 'real'—even if, by *some standard*, it is not the 'real colour' of the car.

All those so-called 'phenomenal qualities' and their antics are real insofar as they play a very basic role in our original concept of 'reality.' What counts as real for us, if not those sensible things with which we are perceptually acquainted? This is not to say that those sensible things are real, where that is a positive claim about the ontological furniture of the world. It is more a conceptual claim concerning what 'real' means. Sensible things constitute one standard among others for what may count as being 'real.' Phenomenal qualities and their antics belong, essentially, to this standard.

What sense does it make to say that what is perceived is in perception *represented* as having the phenomenal qualities it does, if those phenomenal qualities are just part of its reality as something perceived—as a 'sensible thing'? On the correct view, perception is just *the face* of that part of reality that is purely sensible. Thus, *its being perceived is a part of that kind of reality.*

Why should anyone have a different take on the matter? If they do, it is probably because it is so difficult to get rid of the picture according to which there is a gap between mind and world. This is even difficult—perhaps more difficult—when one claims to have overcome the gap, that is, the gap between the 'content of perception' on the one hand and perceived reality on the other. Having failed to scrutinize the (concept of) the perceived closely enough to see the reality it just is, one can wind up believing that that reality must first be conceptualized in order for it to be *made amenable to* perception.

CHAPTER SEVEN

Contextualism or Relativism?

A STRONG EMPHASIS PLACED on context has for a long time been a characteristic feature of Continental philosophy, particularly in its hermeneutical form. On this side of the philosophical divide everything seems to have been about context. So much has this been true that, in the words of my friend Paolo Parrini, there has been reason to doubt whether anything is left to think about *in* context. It is clear that, *precisely in the context of this philosophical tradition*, the emphasis placed on context more often than not comes down to a kind of *relativization*. Very often it was associated with the cliché that 'there are no facts, but only interpretations'—as if the very fact that facts are determined contextually were itself an argument against facts and, furthermore, such determination, on account of its contextuality, necessarily amounted to *interpretation*.

*As a matter of fact it might be that the primary relation between thinking agents and 'context' is *not* interpretive. Furthermore, it might be that far from making facts elusive—or, even less, impossible—contextuality is a condition on grasping any facts at all. However, I am not going to challenge the understanding of context in Continental thought here—an understanding which is, on the whole, hermeneutical. I will instead focus on the notion of context that has been at issue in recent Analytic philosophy. In fact, in so doing we might encounter the same problems—or at least analogous ones.

For some time now contextualism has been very fashionable in Analytic philosophy of language, as well as in other parts of Analytic philosophy. Of course, no one wants to swim in the mainstream, and it is clear that, initially at least, contextualism in Analytic philosophy was a reaction to a 'semantic' mainstream that took meaning to be an objective property of the elements of language and that was independent of their concrete uses in context. However, it is not an exaggeration to say that as far as the philosophy of language is concerned, contextualism has to some extent become the new mainstream. A sure sign of this is that François Recanati, certainly a pivotal figure in contemporary philosophy of language, endorses a form of (moderate) contextualism.[1]

Now, the relative success of contextualism has given rise to misgivings and sparked debate among Analytic philosophers. In certain parts of contemporary Analytic philosophy one often hears it said that contextualism necessarily results in relativism—if it is not already a disguised form of relativism—and thus in the loss of truth and reality. Of course, when a guardian of the Analytic flame says as much, he or she may well have in view the deleterious effects that an emphasis on context has had on Continental philosophy. After all, is it not true that the same cause always produces the same effect?

However, an interesting aspect of the Analytic revival of the problem is that it undoubtedly aids us in distinguishing between *contextualism* and *relativism*. In fact it makes this distinction absolutely necessary, for in the wake of contextualism relativism also appears to have begun a new life in Analytic philosophy—although perhaps to a lesser extent. (Once again, François Recanati, who describes himself as 'a moderate relativist' serves as an example.[2]) Yet this is not to deny that these themes are conflated in Analytic philosophy from time to time.

However, the Analytic treatment of these respective problems gives them a logical form: Firstly, by formulating clearly the question as to whether they are substantially the same and, secondly, by providing a way to distinguish between them.[3] Recent research in

1. See Recanati 2004, for example.
2. See Recanati 2007.
3. Richard 2004 broke the ground here. Stojanovic 2008 provides a very helpful synthesis, and Recanati 2007 maps the debate comprehensively. I am deeply indebted to these three sources.

Analytic philosophy of language therefore allows us explore the logic of contextualism and relativism in a deeper way. We are now perhaps in a position to examine the consequences of the logical distinction that has been drawn between them for the philosophy of language, epistemology, and the philosophy of mind.

What is the logical structure of contextualism and relativism? At first glance, one might think there is a single structure here: Is contextualism not *relativization to a context?* However, some simple examples give a taste of the difference between the two.

A few years ago my doctoral student, Charlotte, spent some time at the University of Chicago. She had the opportunity to give a talk about contextualism, and she used this example: "Before I came here I believed I would be in Chicago. But now, I am spending all my time at the Regenstein Library. All I do is work on my dissertation. So, no, I am not in Chicago!" Her point was that the context in question—being trapped in the Regenstein Library, which essentially looks like a bunker—altered the meaning of 'being in Chicago.'

I did not find this example convincing. It was easy to respond in the following way: "You *are* in Chicago! Your commitment to your dissertation and the fact that you're working for most of the day in a bunker cut off from the external world doesn't diminish this fact. Go out! Get a life! You will see that you are in Chicago."

Of course, her point was that she did not really have the opportunity to truly experience or enjoy Chicago. However, that is not the same as saying: 'I am not in Chicago.' She should have said: 'I'm in Chicago, but am unable to enjoy it,' or, 'I'm in Chicago, but haven't seen much of it.' But by no twist of the imagination can 'not being in Chicago' mean the same as 'being Chicago but not in a position to enjoy the city'; nor can 'being in Chicago' mean the same as 'being in Chicago *and* in a position to enjoy the city.' Of course, I can use this expression to *imply* that I'm in a position to enjoy the city—perhaps by exultantly posting: 'I'm in Chicago!' on Facebook. However, all I *say* in such cases is that I am in Chicago. We should distinguish between what is said and what is implied.

This basic distinction, one made by the advocates of strict semantics—that is to say: semantics unpolluted by pragmatic considerations—should certainly be retained. However, the hard-liners of strict semantics go a bridge too far in thinking that so-called 'literal meaning' is enough to determine the truth-value of what is said. For, as a matter of fact, if 'I am in Chicago' is what is said—and *just* 'I am in Chicago'—then depending on which of the many *ways of being or not being in Chicago* is at stake I either will or won't be in Chicago, and my statement will consequently be either true or false.

This is the whole point of *contextualism*, strictly speaking: if we want to make sense of truth and falsity we need to look for what is concretely at stake in a statement in its determinate context. The idea is not that we should look beyond what is said—for example by including the implicatures of a statement in the assessment of its truth-value, but that *what is said*, not the words we use to say it, has a truth-value. By themselves words do not say anything. *We* say something in using them. Crucially, reference to the context in which we use them is essential to the determination of what we thus do.

Thus contextualism, far from rejecting the distinction between what is said and what is implied, instead forwards a position on 'what is said' according to which it is always said in a *determinate way*, one that presupposes a *particular context*. Contextuality is therefore a perfectly objective feature of *what is said*. As such, if Charlotte says—on some definite understanding of these words—that she is 'in Chicago,' it is not simply up to her whether she is in Chicago or not: the understanding in question *determines* whether or not she is in Chicago, regardless of what her feelings about it may be.

On many understandings of those words the fact that Charlotte is not happy with her stay in Chicago does not change the fact that that's where she is. Of course, in a particular conversation one cannot exclude the possibility that Charlotte is using the words 'being in Chicago' in such a way that it means 'partying in Chicago.' Admittedly, this use would be uncommon. However, using language is—as with any tool—something we *do*, and in some sense there is

no limit to what we can do with language. There is no predetermined list or fixed set of ways of using a word.

Nonetheless, a linguistic usage can only exist insofar as it is able
to be shared—that is, insofar as at least some interlocutors can make
sense of it. As when in conversation someone says: "Oh, that's what
you mean by 'being in Chicago'!" Usually, this sort of acknowledge-
ment goes hand in hand with an ascription of a definite *context* to
the utterance in question, one in which it makes sense to use those
words in that way.

And perhaps one can conceive of particular contexts in which
'Chicago' means 'Chicago the party town.'[4] After all, this is not so
different from such classic examples as: 'London is no longer
London,' where this means it is no longer the party capital of the
world. This utterance has truth-conditions, as shown by the fact
that we can disagree with it. However, what we disagree about
would in this case be completely determined by the particular understanding of 'London' as a party city. Otherwise, it wouldn't even
make sense to say that 'London is no longer London.' The alleged
'literal meaning' does not bring forth falsity here, only sheer nonsense. However, in context the utterance can, on some understanding, still make sense.

Now, regarding Charlotte's statement, the relevant question is
just this: Is she using the phrase 'being in Chicago' in such a way
that working in the Regenstein Library is incompatible with being
in Chicago? It seems doubtful that she is. What she means is obvious: this is not what she believed or expected being in Chicago
would be like. Of course, that alone does not make it false to say
that she's in Chicago. To some extent, when she says: 'Finally, I'm
not in Chicago!' her utterance in fact presupposes that the opposite
of what she says is true. Like most examples of irony, it only works
insofar as it somehow affirms what it denies. As long as we fail to

---

4. Think, for example, of the use of the names 'Dakar,' 'Tokyo,' etc. in a Modern
Talking music video.

understand that she is actually in Chicago, we will not understand what she is saying.

However, another strategy is still possible if we want to leave irony out of the picture. Perhaps we can say that *objectively* Charlotte is in Chicago. This, however, is not how she sees things. The particular position in which she finds herself does not meet her standard for what it is to be in Chicago. Thus, *by her own assessment*, she is not in Chicago.

This might sound similar to the previous solution that consisted in introducing an understanding of the phrase 'being in Chicago' according to which being stuck in the Regenstein Library *does not count as* being in Chicago. However, from a logical perspective it works differently. According to the present interpretation, Charlotte should certainly be willing to acknowledge that it is perfectly possible to say that she is in Chicago, thereby endorsing an understanding of the phrase according to which being in the Regenstein Library is a way of being in Chicago. Nevertheless, she still wants to make the point that this is not *what she counts as being in Chicago*. Thus, the point no longer seems to be about meaning but about the kind of reality *you* count as satisfying a given meaning.

We should note that the fact that the standard of assessment here is subjective—that is, *the way Charlotte looks at things*—does not entail that we cannot make sense of it or objectify it. We can perfectly well say that: "Of course, given Charlotte's expectations, this is not Chicago!" However, we should probably still draw a distinction between *Charlotte's standard* and what 'being in Chicago' *means:* even in Charlotte's mouth 'being in Chicago' better not *mean* anything like 'not being in the Regenstein Library,' if her point is to be intelligible. It seems that everything hinges on Charlotte's judgment about what counts as a correct match between, on the one hand, the meaning of this particular expression in these circumstances and, on the other hand, reality.

Now, there are varied ways of making sense of the peculiar character of such judgments. Firstly, one might think Charlotte simply mistaken. For instance, she was kidnapped when she arrived at O'Hare, blindfolded, and taken directly to the Regenstein Library, where she is now imprisoned. Thus, she is in Chicago—and would endorse a perfectly ordinary understanding of what 'being in Chicago' is—but simply does not know that *she is in Chicago*. In fact, as with anything else, there might be many ways to be mistaken about this. Of course, this does not change the fact that *Charlotte is in Chicago.*

Secondly, one might think that Charlotte assesses the claim that she is in Chicago according to a standard that qualifies it. In which case, it might be that unless her 'being in Chicago' attains, in her view, a certain intensity or quality, it does not deserve to be called 'being in Chicago.' If so, we could speak, from outside as it were, of Charlotte's perspective having a *subjective bias* concerning the conditions under which someone can be said to 'be in Chicago.' This is what relativism is all about: *biases*, whether subjective or otherwise. *Strong relativism* holds that there is no truth independent of such biases.

There is something fishy about this position. It appears to entail an internal contradiction: a bias alters the perception of a truth, or even the truth itself, making true what was not true *per se*; however, in one way or another, the very notion of a bias always presupposes a picture of truth as something that—at least at a preliminary stage—is independent of *any* bias. As such, the idea that truth is intrinsically biased—which philosophical relativism often comes down to—seems to be inconsistent.

Of course, there might be cleverer formulations of relativism which elude this criticism and that, perhaps, even do justice to the kernel of truth in relativism—if indeed there is one, as certainly its popularity makes it tempting to think there is. However, I am neither going to explore this issue further, nor attempt to discuss relativism as such. Instead I am going to focus on the logical difference between the kind of position that I have just presented and *contextualism.*

Is it ever the case that to be in Hyde Park (where the Regenstein Library stands) is *objectively*—that is, independently of any 'subjective bias'—to not be in Chicago? When I take the Metra from 57th Street station in Hyde Park—that is, the station on the 57th south street *of Chicago*—I can see a sign on the platform that says 'Chicago,' and which features an arrow that strongly implies we are not in Chicago already. It is a bit like when you arrive at Narita airport in Tokyo: On one side there is a sign that says 'Asia,' and on the other one that says 'Japan.' Of course this case is fairly straightforward. It is easy to make sense of the fact that on some understandings Japan is counted as a part of Asia and that, on others, it is contrasted to the continent considered to be the 'real' Asia. It all depends on what one means by Asia or, more precisely, what kind of distinction one has in view.

The same goes for Chicago. If I am interested in administrative matters, Hyde Park is certainly a part of the city of Chicago—even if this was not always the case. However, it is perfectly understandable that, in certain circumstances, for example when taking the train, Chicago is only downtown Chicago. It certainly makes sense for me to say that 'I'm going to Chicago,' when I ride the inbound Metra from Hyde Park. This is a public usage, one instituted by the train company, and as such is perfectly understandable. Of course, in order to make sense, it requires a little *context*—taking the train in order to escape from Hyde Park, for instance.

So, what counts as 'Chicago' from a certain point of view will not count as 'Chicago' from *every* point of view. It does not depend on subjective standards of assessment, but on objectively different things that we can mean by 'Chicago.' Now the fact that we mean this or that, so that *this* rather than *that* is relevant to the question whether we are currently in Chicago or not, clearly depends on the context: Are we boarding an inbound train? Or are we participating in the census? Each situation—and each practice—establishes a definite meaning for the phrase 'being in Chicago.' Or perhaps it would be more accurate to say: a definite *understanding*, if we want to distinguish between linguistic meaning—the lexical meanings of words, as might be found in the dictionary—and the referential capacity of speech: our capacity to exert a grip on reality by using given words in a definite way—a way not found 'in' those words themselves.

The fact that in this case everything seems to hinge on administrative conventions helps us to make sense of the 'objectivity' of the relevant understanding. It is not up to the subject to understand things one way or another. She has to enter the game and understand *what it is about.* In this way she also understands how 'Chicago,' for example, is being meant.

However, the contextual determination of meaning is not necessarily conventional. There cannot be a convention for every situation and indeed there is not. If you ask me whether I have ever been to Madrid, I suppose I should say 'no.' As a matter fact I once had a connecting flight at Bajaras on a trip to Sevilla. But does Bajaras international airport count as 'Madrid' in a conversation we're having about the cities we've visited? Probably not.

But, consider John, an airline pilot, whose colleague asks him, in a professional context: "Have you ever been to Madrid?" This might unequivocally mean: "Have you ever been to Madrid airport?" (i.e., Bajaras). Of course, *there is no convention here.* But there is the topic of the discourse as well as some background: a shared practice, or at least a practice into which it is possible to project oneself. If John the pilot says to me: "No, so far, I have not been to Madrid." I can also understand: "So far, I have never landed a plane in Bajaras," if the context calls for it—although I am no pilot.

There is certainly no specific convention here. (Nor anything automatic about it: a pilot can also go on vacation, and so 'go to Madrid' in the more common sense of the expression.) Nobody has ever settled it that 'going to Madrid,' under certain specific circumstances, means: 'using Bajaras airport.' However, the lack of a convention does not make such an understanding, when it is relevant, any less 'objective.' Once you have understood what is at stake there is no problem of assessment, nor is it up to you to decide arbitrarily whether John has ever been to Madrid or not.

Thus, contextualism is a principle of objectivity, rather than a relativism understood as 'subjectivism,' for the role of the context is *to fix the content, not to make it unstable.* The whole point of contextualism is understanding, of any given situation, 'what it is about.'

Now, an Analytic philosopher who defends relativism might object that it need not necessarily entail either 'subjectivism' or arbitrariness. After all, if relativism is just about assessing the truth-value of content according to *standards,* there is no reason to think it necessarily entails subjectivism. Quite the opposite, if the standard has been set up objectively. Depending on which of a diverse range of standards is used, a given content will be sometimes true and sometimes false. But this much is objective: according to a specific standard, there is normally no doubt about the truth-value of the content.

It is very tempting to treat the contextualist point along these lines, that is, as a particular case of 'objective' relativity. And, indeed, it is common practice to do so.[5] After all, haven't we said that *contextualism is concerned with relativity to context?*

I believe that, below this surface appearance, there remains a genuine gulf between the perspectives. One should firstly ask: *Relativity of what?* One should also delve deeper into the logic of contextualism. It may well turn out that it is not about *relativity* at all.

If, provisionally, we take contextualism to entail a kind of relativity—relativity to context—we should make clear that it is *content* that is supposed to be relative to context, *not* truth-value. The truth-value depends precisely on the content—no additional factor is involved. On the other hand, what is usually called 'relativism' is not

5. See for instance Kölbel 2008, p. 27.

concerned with content but rather *the truth-value of content*; it holds that truth-value may vary, whilst content remains the same.

Thus, on one side there is relativity of content. On the other, relativity of truth-value (where the content is fixed and so no longer relative—or at least *not anymore relative*, the issue of its relativity to context having already been settled). These are, of course, two different topics. Nevertheless, as the former appears to constitute a form of relativity as much as the latter, aren't we permitted to think of it as a kind of 'relativism'? Why should relativism be subject to a 'specialization' that narrows it down to the relativity *of truth-value*?

To this kind of question there is generally nothing to say except, "Well, terminology is a matter of choice; if you want to call it 'relativism,' why not?" However, if someone means to suggest a substantial analogy by using the same term in each case—in effect suggesting that the same kind of 'relativity' exists on both sides, but concerning different things or operating at different 'levels'—then the matter may prove to be more complex. For upon closer inspection it seems doubtful whether there is any relativity in the first case which corresponds to the kind found in the second.

In order to understand this, we must once again consider the logical structure of relativism. It is a general characteristic of relativism to posit something that is invariant and then to make room for variation in relation to it—indeed, this is precisely what 'relativity' consists in. For example, relativism about truth-value assumes that there is something that can bear one or another truth-value depending on the standard of assessment in question. Relativism regarding truth-value does not question the identity and stability of that 'something.' On the contrary, it takes it for granted. This is why I said that strictly speaking the problem relativism (about truth-value) is concerned with arises only once the issue of content has been settled.

Of course, it seems that one can be both a contextualist and a relativist. In fact, most relativists are—thereby combining, in some sense, two kinds of relativity. However, it is worth observing that proponents of full-blooded contextualism are usually *not* relativists. Why is this? It is probably because the logical structure of relativism presupposes precisely that which contextualism continually criticizes: *absolute propositions (truth-bearers) that exist independently of any context.*

In order to get to grips with this point, we can take a look at what was the original model for logical relativism: *temporalism.* (We might also have considered François Recanati's treatment of modalities.) Temporalism consists in introducing 'temporal propositions.' Temporal propositions are not propositions whose content is temporal. They are propositions that are such that the truth-value of their content changes over time. Today I can say: 'I am in Leipzig,' just as I might also have said it yesterday. Within the classical Fregean framework the proposition expressed in the former case is that I am in Leipzig on a certain day (i.e., the day of this very utterance); in the latter case *another proposition is expressed* to the effect that I am in Leipzig on the day of *that* utterance (i.e., yesterday). One proposition happens to be true; the other false.

Temporalism, on the other hand, holds that both utterances, though made on different days, express *the same proposition.* Namely, that I am in Leipzig. However, this proposition is true in one case and false in another. As such the distinctive feature of temporalism—more generally of logical 'relativism,' of which temporalism is the paradigm case—is that it disconnects propositional content from its truth-value. It holds that content can remain constant even as its truth-value changes. It therefore assumes that there exists a gap between content and truth-value. As such, content may not be enough to go on.

Now, this is precisely what contextualism calls into question. The whole point of contextualism is that *a content that does not admit of being judged is no content at all.* As a matter of fact, contextualism is first and foremost a point about *the fine-grained nature of propositional content.* According to contextualism there is no such proposition: 'I am in Leipzig' where that means: 'I am in Leipzig at a certain time,' if that does not already include the specification of this certain time. The proposition that 'I am in Leipzig at a certain time,' if undated, amounts to nothing. It is not a determinate thing. It is not assessable, but only because, as such, it does not mean anything—not anything determinate therefore not anything.

*Of course, the real contextualist point is that, in some particular circumstances, this utterance may nevertheless be perfectly meaningful. If, seeing Andrea in Chicago, I ask her: 'Which university do you work at?,' or simply: '*Where are you?*,' she can legitimately answer me by saying: 'I am in Leipzig,' thereby meaning: 'In general, I am in Leipzig; I live and work there.' Of course, this does not amount to asserting that, in saying 'I am in Leipzig' she means: 'I am in Leipzig' timelessly, and that she thereby asserts a content that can take on a different truth-value depending on the occasion of utterance. When someone says that he / she is in Leipzig *in general*, he / she says *something different* than that he / she is in Leipzig at a very definite time, one that happens to be the time of the utterance. To say that one is in Leipzig when one is currently there, does not amount to saying that one 'is in Leipzig' timelessly—something which must then be assessed according to the *punctual* time at which it is said, or to which it is applied.[6]

The difference between the sort of relativism I am discussing (for this term might be used to describe many other things) and contextualism, is that it is essential to the contextualist view that there is nothing which is said or thought that lacks determination (although, of course, there is an incredible variety of determinations in what is said and some might look indeterminate by the standards of others). More generally, nothing that can be said or thought stops short of its own application. Of course, not every content is temporally determined. However, when a content is not, it does not for that reason *lack* temporal determination. It just *doesn't require* it.

6. The need for distinguishing between the two, and of making room for the second, are important points made by Recanati 2007.

Contextualism stems from a tradition according to which *there is no such thing as half-content:* if there is content then it is fully determined. Its conditions of application are as determinate as can be. Fully-fledged content involves a claim about some state of affairs: it determines how things should be if the utterance or thought that has / is such content is to be satisfied. This is precisely the reason why, according to contextualism, we should take the context into account: we need to if we want to deal with content whose bearing on reality is clear, namely, *genuine content.* Genuine content is necessarily contextual in the sense that it is only in context that something like genuine content can be articulated. What is to be found in context is 'the very point' of what is said—'what it is about.' *No content is without point:* aboutness is an intrinsic feature of content, and, as such, it cannot remain sketchy or blurred. If it does, then it is not genuine content, but only something that *looks like content*—what Frege would have called a *Scheingedanke.*

Viewed from this perspective, not only are the respective logical structures of relativism and contextualism completely different, they also cannot endorse the same philosophy of mind. The 'contents' posited by relativism do not exist on the contextualist view, or if they do they are not genuine ones. According to contextualism there cannot be the gap between content and truth-value (filled in by 'standards of assessment' such as 'at the present time') that relativism requires. Dealing with content involves dealing with a determinate take on the world that is assessable *per se. Contents themselves are contextual*—but this is a different story.

The outcome of all this is that it now appears incredibly difficult to interpret contextualism in terms of 'relativity.' For *what is relative to what?* As we said earlier, an apparently natural answer to this question is: content is relative to context. However, on further examination, this answer proves to be incorrect, or at least problematic. For a consequence of what we have just said is that *content is not relative so much as it is contextual.* That is to say, to some extent, 'context' is part of content. There is no content independent of, or upstream from, context.

Now, one might say: "Indeed, content does not itself allow for relativity, but what is relative is the fact that our utterance or thought has / is this or that 'content.'" Yet this is the whole point: on such a view, one goes on considering context as some *additional factor*, which, when added to something, produces a determinate 'content.' The question is: *added to what?* What necessitates this complement that relativity to context allegedly calls for?

The problem is that in order for the story concerning 'relativity' to make sense, there needs to be *something that is not yet a content, but that can become one within a given context.* Is this not exactly what contextualism contests? More precisely, contextualism denies, even if such a thing exists, that it can in any way serve as content. On the contextualist view, there are no 'proto-contents'—that is, contents that are not full-blooded, lack contextual determination, or that remain unclear in their application.

Of course, there still remain the words themselves or to put it more precisely, 'the words by themselves.' The whole point of con-textualism is that words by themselves have a *linguistic meaning* (that is what makes them 'words'), but not a semantic value—they do not have *content* in the sense in which philosophers use this term: they do not say, *by themselves,* anything about how things are *(and therefore they just do not say anything). We* say things *with* them—many things, in fact—and we do so in specific contexts that bear on *what we say.* As such, what some given words express certainly seems to be context-relative. So we finally seem to have found the locus of 'relativity' in contextuality.

However, we should observe that such relativity is, so to speak, only relative when viewed 'from outside.' Whenever words are used, they are used in context on a definite understanding of them. To be sure, it might turn out to be difficult for an outsider to identify this understanding at first. Getting at meaning-in-context can even prove to be a complex hermeneutical task. However, for the agents inside the situation there is usually no problem. They do not have to interpret the words; they are *using them.* At the level of *use,* there is no room for relativity. Just as there are no 'half-contents,' there are no 'half-used' words. To put the point in the terminology of the *Tractatus:* what is relative is the meaning of *signs (Zeichen),* not of *symbols (Symbole,* i.e., signs as they are used). Use determines meaning as perfectly as it needs to.

However, if by themselves signs essentially have *no meaning,* does it make sense to say that their meaning is 'relative'? After all, contextuality might not be a matter of relativity *at all,* even at the so-called 'linguistic level.'

On the other hand, we should consider what happens to 'thoughts.' If we assume, following the Fregean tradition, that a thought is just what is expressed by a genuinely descriptive utterance—I mean an utterance where circumstances are fit for description—then we clearly cannot apply the kind of relativization to them that we have to 'what is said' (independently of the fact that we have shown the limits of such 'relativization'). For what would play the part of 'simple signs' *(bloße Zeichen)* in the case of thoughts, which themselves *are* contents?

A good principle by which to distinguish between language and mind might be that wherever there is language, signs are involved, whereas thoughts are expressed by (used) signs, but are not themselves signs. This is a *grammatical* distinction capturing the way we use the word 'thought.' No substantial ontological claim about the nature of thought is hereby made. The point is just that it makes no sense to ask which thought a particular thought *expresses.*

It is therefore very difficult to know *what has a relative value* in the case of thought. To some degree it makes sense to say that, depending on the context, given words take on different meanings and thereby express *different thoughts.* However, we shall not in turn discover what in thoughts might be said 'to take one meaning or another,' for thought *is* meaning (or can at least play this part) without *having* meaning. Of course, there is no shortage of ingenious philosophers who have tried to introduce something into thought that can play the part of the *'to be interpreted' signs* that we find in linguistic contextualism (if we buy its mild relativist interpretation). What we wind up with then, are something like the *stubs* or, to put it more 'syntactically,' the *radicals* of thoughts.

Now, the upshot of contextualism for the philosophy of mind—a *prima facie* linguistic thesis which turns out to be about *the fine-grained nature of thoughts*—is that there are no stubs or radicals. Or, if there are, *they are not thoughts*. Thus, the divergence between relativism and contextualism ultimately hinges on a difference of conception regarding what a *thought* is. On a certain conception of what a thought is, it is possible to interpret the contextuality of thoughts in terms of 'relativity.' On another conception—one that strict contextualism seems to endorse—it is not.

So behind the different philosophies of language one finds, as ever, different philosophies of mind.

Now, in order to avoid having neglected something, the previous analysis will require a codicil. I have pretended that the form of generality that relativism (understood on the model of temporalism) ascribes to the expressed content is simply incompatible with contextualism. I think in some ways it is. Nevertheless, it is possible to make sense of relativism within the contextualist framework. It can even be said that the kernel of truth in relativism can only be clearly made out *within this framework*.

The point is as follows. As Max Kölbel puts it, according to temporalism "the sentence 'It is Monday' can be seen to express the same, *tensed* proposition, whenever it is used. This proposition is true on Mondays only, and false on other days."[7] I have disputed that this is *always* the case by making the point that often 'It is Monday' just means: it is Monday *this very day*. This is not only *true* if it is Monday today, but *means it*—or at least it should be *understood* thus.

The question then is: Why should we be tempted to think the sentence 'It is Monday' expresses *the same thought* when it is uttered on

7. Kölbel 2008, p. 2.

different days? Apparently it is because this sentence *can be used with different purposes and in different ways.* In some contexts, the speaker may just want to tell the date; in others she might want to emphasize that the present day belongs to *a class of days.* For instance: 'It is Monday' (and so, for example, we are eating vegetables at the mensa). In the second case, the speaker's affirmation involves a kind of generality: one might think 'the same' about many other days—in theory, an infinite series of them. The point seems to be precisely that when I think of today that it is Monday, I am thinking exactly the same thing as I was when I thought it of last Monday. In other words, the *topic* of a thought might be the singularity of this Monday, as well as the *commonality* of Mondays.

Still, we should distinguish *the topic of a thought* and its *object:* the target of its *aboutness.* So long as such a thought has not been applied to a specific day, it is neither true nor false, so, according to the Fregean definition, it is no thought. A real, full-blooded thought is about something, and thus *makes a difference.* On this view each time I think 'the same' thing about different days, those are, in fact, different thoughts—although their content consists in thinking those days are, from a certain perspective, 'the same.' It is like when we say: 'I think the same about you as I do about him.' Those are not 'the same thought.' To think the same about someone as you do about someone else, is to think two different thoughts. However, the alleged identity of 'what is thought' in either case is then an important part of the way we think about both objects.

This outcome might tempt us to analyse these thoughts as having a 'content' devoid of any definite aboutness, and that can be applied to different objects. This picture very likely confuses *thought* and *concept.* Concepts won't be thoughts, but rather something into which it is possible, under certain circumstances, to analyse thoughts. For instance, I might assess whether or not this day satisfies the concept of Monday—as a matter of fact, it might even be a Monday from some point of view and yet not satisfy that concept according to the way we're currently using it: for instance, roast is being served at the mensa! However, the thought that I entertain is still about *this* day. The fact that I characterize this day as satisfying or failing to satisfy a general condition, does not mean that the full-blooded general thought I entertain is not about this day. There is plenty of room for ascribing various conceptual structures to given thoughts—depending, in particular, on the other thoughts we compare them to—but there is no room for a relativist understanding of each particular thought.

Nevertheless, it is clear that, so understood—and so defused, so to speak—the relativist analysis can help us make sense of *a real contextual difference:* a difference of understanding that our utterances might call for, depending on the generality with which they are targeting the object they are about.

CHAPTER EIGHT

Contextualism without Representationalism

THE TITLE of this chapter may come as a surprise, for it is in danger of seeming trivial. It seems obvious that, of all contemporary philosophical doctrines, contextualism would be the one that is at odds with representationalism. Doesn't the latter amount to ascribing *intrinsic* furniture to the mind—that is, items that are what they are independently of context, even if their surfacing in the mind is *triggered* by a given context? Conversely, contextualism considers the very idea of such *intrinsic furniture* problematic. This is why, in his masterwork in the philosophy of mind,[1] Charles Travis develops a fully-fledged criticism of the notion of representation as a consequence of his radical contextualist view in the philosophy of language.

For all that, the observation that contextualism and representationalism are opposed might not be a trivial one. Contextualism originally belonged to the philosophy of language, whereas the concept of 'representation' is much more a part of the philosophy of mind. Why should a claim that belongs primarily to the philosophy of language conflict with a conceptual framework characteristic of a particular philosophy of mind? It seems this is only possible if *some counterpart to linguistic contextualism can be found for the mind.* Yet what could the mental counterpart to the phenomenon of linguistic contextuality be? The answer to this question is far from clear. There may even be a pitfall lurking in the idea of a 'counterpart.'

In this chapter, I would like to show (i) that contextualism about language also sheds light on how the mind works; (ii) that to some

1. Travis 2000.

degree it makes sense to call the mind's furniture 'contextual'; and that (iii) despite this, the contextualist claim as articulated in the philosophy of language cannot be straightforwardly transposed into the philosophy of mind, but rather needs to be rearticulated.

I would like to emphasize the following ostensible paradox (perhaps merely ostensible if *contextualism* is true): the *literal* transposition of linguistic contextualism to the level of the mind leads to *representationalism* and thus, to some extent, the opposite of contextualism. Finding an adequate formulation for contextualism in relation to the mind is not so trivial a task. As a matter of fact, a further inquiry into the contextualist claim—understood as the general philosophical thesis it is—can teach us as much about the basic asymmetry between the grammar of language and the grammar of mind as it does about the solidarity that exists between them.

LINGUISTIC CONTEXTUALISM

In order to formulate the problem correctly, we should first remind ourselves of the basics of linguistic contextualism.

Contextualism about language is the idea that, in order to assess a linguistic performance, one must take its context into account. Different kinds of linguistic performances call for different dimensions of assessment. Thus, the contextualist thesis can be formulated in a very general way. However, it is clear that in standard contextualism, the reference to *truth* and *falsity* is pivotal. The fact that a sentence has no truth-value by itself, but only acquires one *when it is used on a particular occasion*, sheds light on the general contextuality of speech acts and their various dimensions of accomplishment.

As far as truth is at stake, the minimal formulation of linguistic contextualism has it that the truth-value of what is said depends on the context. Now, the question is: What is 'the context'? An example can help us get to grips with the problem. If I say: 'There is milk in the fridge,' the sentence I utter has a truth-value only if the fridge in question is a particular specified fridge. Now, often, when I utter such a sentence, it is about the fridge currently right in front of us, or at least in the flat we are currently in. As such, the identity of this fridge—and therefore of *what is really said*, and thus *the truth-value of what is said*—is determined by the context.

Of course there are situations in which the fridge in question need not be present to the speaker, as for example when we mean *the fridge we normally talk about*, in which case the reference is specified by the habits of the speaker or, more precisely, the shared habits of the speaker and the hearer.

There are also situations in which the reference is specified by what is present to the *hearer* rather than the speaker. For instance, I am talking on the phone to Simon, and he asks me where the milk is. I reply: 'The milk is in the fridge,' referring to the fridge that *Simon* can see. Building on an insight of Charles J. Fillmore's, François Recanati has thoroughly investigated these phenomena of perspectival anchoring. Whether the perspective is that of the speaker at the very time of his speech act or any other, in all such cases the point is that, without the specification of this perspective, it is impossible to know what the sentence used is about, and it is therefore impossible to ascribe any truth-value to what is said.

Now, this *perspectivism* is a weak, watered-down form of contextualism. It comes down to a generalization of what is usually called 'indexical contextualism.' In a proposition, the indexical element introduces a reference to something that should be taken from the context—generally from the context of utterance, but some shifts of perspective are also conceivable at this level. In the sentence 'the milk is in the fridge,' *either* one can say that the definite article in '*the* fridge' has a deictic function and is a kind of demonstrative, *or* one can say that the proposition expressed as a whole has a kind of *unarticulated constituent*: some kind of implicit 'here,' as in 'It is raining (here).'

However, *radical contextualism*, as advocated by Charles Travis, has something else in view. *Indexical contextualism*, even when generalized, just makes the point that sometimes the content expressed by some words is logically *incomplete* (i.e., not such that it can be true or false) and that we have to find in the context (either of the utterance or of the perspective created by the utterance) an additional factor that renders it complete. That contextualism, however, presupposes that the content, for the most part, is independent of the context. On such a view the content takes from the context only what it needs.

Radical contextualism, on the other hand, holds that the content is *absolutely* dependent on the context. For the context does not simply provide an additional factor that helps stabilize the truth-value of what is meant, but precisely determines *what is meant*. Thus, if for example I say: 'There is milk in the fridge,' then depending on the circumstances, it can mean something along the lines of: 'If you look for some milk to drink, there is a bottle in the fridge,' or: 'Be careful when cleaning the fridge; there is spilt milk in it.' (This example is Charles Travis's.) These are definitely two very different ways for some milk to be in the fridge. However, *the words by themselves do not say which of these ways is in question.* They say that only insofar as they are used in a definite context. This case is different from the previous one. The meaning does not require an *additional element* which varies depending on the context in order to be made complete. Depending on the context we have *two completely different meanings*, pure and simple.

Of course it only makes sense to say this if by 'meaning' we understand something that *bears on the world:* meaning in the sense of *meaning that things are a certain way*. From this point of view we get, in the second case, a very different meaning on each understanding of the given sentence. To some extent this is true in the first case as well: depending on *which fridge* is in question the sentence certainly will not 'mean' the same thing. However, one can nevertheless say in this case that the sentence, on different occasions, 'says the same thing' about different fridges. Thus, on a certain interpretation of what 'meaning' is, it is possible to say that the 'meaning' does not change in this example: some *general structure of meaning* is at least preserved. That is the whole point of *indexicality*. In the *radical contextualist example*, things are different. Depending on the context, we are confronted with substantially different meanings.

ACONTEXTUAL MIND?

Now what is true of language is not necessarily true of mind. This is the case even if we uphold the Fregean connection between them according to which a thought is that which can be expressed in a sentence (if, that is, certain conditions are met regarding the sentence and the speech act in which it is used). As a matter of fact, it is precisely the problem of context that seems to provide a possible point of departure for a differentiation of language and mind.

It is very tempting to say that the fact that a linguistic sequence expresses *this* or *that content* is contextual—that this is precisely what contextuality is about—but that 'content' itself is not contextual. For how could it be? On this conception, to understand an expression-in-context amounts to a kind of *selection* between different available meanings that exist—or, at least, are what they are—independently of the context. These meanings are in no way contextual themselves. However, depending on the context, we can activate one or another of them. What is contextual is the connection between language and thought—not thought itself.

Of course, one is not obliged to buy into the Platonic metaphysics that such an analysis seemingly presupposes: as if thought were, so to speak, *transcendent* to language, and contextuality were merely the visible effect of the contingent linkage between both dimensions. One can alternatively say that the difference between each side is a *difference of category* and that to ascribe to the mind the kind of contextuality that language possesses is a *category mistake.* One does not find elements of the same kind on both sides. This is not to say that those on one side lack some property that those on the other side possess, for example, contextuality. The point is that it is merely *senseless* to compare them. Thoughts cannot be positively characterized as *timeless acontextual entities*. It simply *makes no sense* to think of them as being 'contextual' in the same way that the value of a linguistic performance is.

As a matter of fact, I think that this position is very close to the truth. However, if we leave it at this, we are in danger of missing something: the sense in which *thoughts themselves can be described as contextual*—albeit in a different way than the value of linguistic performances can be. Let us therefore us ask once again: In what sense can a thought be said to be 'contextual'?

MENTAL INDEXICAL CONTEXTUALISM?

François Recanati, particularly in *Perspectival Thought*, did much to extend the idea of context-dependence to thought. However, in beginning to address this issue, he warns us that regarding mind, this might be absolutely *trivial*. For, he says, it is widely accepted that 'representations' in the mind, or at least a good part of them, depend on the world's causal action on the mind. In this sense, thoughts are trivially 'contextual,' whereas the *conventionality* of linguistic tools might have raised doubts about the contextuality of linguistic meaning.

However, if we want to transpose the contextualist claim from the philosophy of language to the philosophy of mind, we should pay attention to the fact that a linguistic performance is not said to be contextual just because it is *triggered* by some specific environment, but because some particular features of that environment should be taken into account when assessing it. This performance is contextual because its *value* depends on the environment—or, more precisely, on the relevant features of the environment: the *context*.

Thus, if we want to extend the contextualist claim to the mind, it appears that we need the elements of mind, that is, the so-called 'thoughts,' to have some *value*. The contextualist claim should be that, in this domain too, the value depends on some distinguished features—and probably some *structuring*—of the environment that we call 'the context.'

Now, it is not very difficult to ascribe values to elements of the mind if they are 'thoughts.' If we stick to a Fregean understanding of what a thought is, then by definition it has a value: a *truth-value*. However, it is not very clear how this truth-value could depend on an external factor like a context. If we are to remain Fregean hard-liners, thoughts must *intrinsically* possess a truth-value. Once you have the thought, there is nothing you can add to it in order to get a truth-value, for the latter depends entirely on the former.

Thus, if we want to claim that there is a contextuality of thought we must as it were *incorporate the context into it as an ingredient*. It should play a role in *the determination of the thought itself*, not in the ascription of a truth-value to it. Yet how can context bear on thought itself?

One solution, which is largely endorsed by Recanati,[2] consists in transposing *indexical contextualism* to the mind. Indeed, talk of 'mental indexicality' has become commonplace.

Let us suppose that I am at a clothing store, rummaging about in a pile of sweaters. At some point, I say: 'This sweater is red,' pointing at an item. A bit later I say: 'This sweater is red,' pointing at another item. The objective meaning of what I say is different each time, because the indexical 'this,' as a pointer, points to a different thing each time, and this pointing contributes to determining the expression's meaning, that is, *to what is said about the world* when using it. According to indexical contextualism, in such a case the context-dependence is located in the deictic. If you do not know which object the speaker is pointing at, or at least *concerning which object* she is using the word 'this,' you do not know what exactly is being said. The deictic brings in the external factor required in order to complete the meaning. There are diverse analyses of how this works but, in general, every analysis of linguistic indexicality draws, in

2. Though his position should in no way be reduced to this. It has much more to do with the notion of *perspective*, of which there is a very sophisticated treatment in Recanati 2007.

one way or another, a distinction between the non-indexical compo-
nent of the sentence's meaning that is derived from the sentence's
mere *words*—if such things exist—and the information taken from
the world that is required to complete that meaning (i.e., such that it
can have *a truth-value*).The idea is that every time I say 'This sweater
is red' I to some extent say the 'same thing.' However, I can say that
'same thing' about different sweaters. Thus, from another point of
view, it is not really 'the same thing.' A different state of affairs
makes each of these utterances true. The deictic singles out what
the statement is about, and thus *fixes what is said*.

Now, the question is: *Do we need anything at the mental level
that fixes what is thought?* Upon hearing some words, you can generally sense when a piece of information is *missing*, and that you
need to look toward the world in order to understand what is being
said. If you have not correctly interpreted the indexical term, you do
not really know what is being said. And in order to interpret it correctly, you need to know what portion of the world it is pointing toward. Only then can you know what the sentence is about. However, when we turn to *thought*, the situation appears to be completely
different. For, at least on some standard conception, if you entertain
a thought, *you usually know what it is about*. Maybe there are 'indexical thoughts,' that is, thoughts about singular things, our relation to which is adequately captured through an act of pointing—
things that we think of *demonstratively*, as it were. We can probably
make sense of something like this. However, in such cases, the *de-
ixis* needn't be *added* to the thought in question: it is, so to speak,
part of it. The thought I entertain is about something definite—and
perhaps even *demonstratively so*. It does not need to be completed in
order to be this. It just is what it is. There is nothing in it that is am-
biguous or underdetermined. If there is then it is not a thought after
all—not a *truth-assessable content*.

In itself the idea of a demonstrative thought raises many difficult
issues: What could it be to demonstrate something 'in thought'? It
seems clear that we should resist the image of a little hand in the

mind that renders a given thought demonstrative by mentally pointing at something. There are no demonstrations except the *real ones* that utilize the tools and devices of demonstration. Nevertheless, we can still make sense of there being a class of thoughts that are expressed in canonical uses of demonstrative sentences. It does not seem outrageous to describe thoughts of this kind as 'demonstrative,' for this captures one of their distinctive features.

Now, the point is that if it does make sense to apply categories to the mind which were initially earned through the study of language—for example, by speaking of 'demonstrative thoughts' in the same way that we speak of 'demonstrative sentences'—we should nevertheless be careful not to push this transposition to the point where it is simply a parallelism, at least not a literal one.

The problem is that, at the mental level, it is difficult to see what the *indexical element* could be. It definitely makes some sense to say that a thought expressible by a particular sort of use of an indexical sentence is 'indexical.' The indexicality *of thought* could then also be connected to the fact that the thinker stands in—or at least projects—*some relation to the designated object*, and that this relation plays a role in the very content of the thought entertained. However, there is no real evidence that this relation must be represented by a particular constituent of the thought: the '(mental) indexical element.' Only an understanding of thought as a kind of super-language would tempt us to say this.

Now, this kind of understanding suffers from multiple problems. The most obvious takes the form of a *regress ad infinitum*. If there are indexical mental items, then they in turn call for an interpretation. The question arises: What does my mental *'this'* designate in context? It seems that behind the first thought there must stand another which interprets it. But why should this thought differ substantially from the first by lacking indexical terms? Put differently, if thought itself functions like a language, which thoughts does this language express?

If one makes the point that thought is indeed a language, *but not one that itself expresses thoughts*—that it is a language that just *is* thought—then we are left with the difficulty of making sense of a language that does not express thoughts. For, on a natural understanding of what language is, reference to thought as something categorically different from it—and that is *expressed* by it—is essential to its definition.

Now, the difficulties resulting from the (perhaps overly direct) attempt to transpose linguistic indexical contextualism to the level of the mind may help us make better sense of the more global difficulty of transposing contextualism to 'the mental level.' The problem seems to be as follows. Contextualism emphasizes context, but without the idea of something that is *in context* the notion of context lacks any sense. This is relatively clear in the case of linguistic performances: *words* are used in context. Thus, if we want to transpose the contextualist paradigm to the level of the mental on the basis of a strict parallelism with linguistic contextualism, we will require a *mental equivalent to words*. Now, there exist such equivalents in the tradition. They are just what are termed 'representations.' Thus, it might seem that, in the final analysis, *contextualism about the mind* and *representationalism* go hand in hand.

To be sure, linguistic contextualism may call for a philosophy of mind that does not consist in a *strict* form of representationalism. On some interpretation of linguistic contextuality there is something left, once I have singled out the representations that are supposed to correspond to words, which depends on a nonrepresentational relation to the world—something like a causal relation, or perhaps direct acquaintance. However, in that case contextualism about mental content will hold that there are *representations* that can be placed in the very context in which the mind allegedly entertains these nonrepresentational relations. *To limit the reach of representations is not to deny that there are representations*, nor that the mind essentially consists in them. Quite the opposite, in fact.

Perhaps *indexical contextualism* does not provide us with an adequate model for *mental contextuality*. In fact things looks slightly different if we focus on *non-indexical contextualism*, for this form of contextualism does not rest on the idea of either an alteration or a complementation of an already given meaning. Of course, words have meaning on their own: 'lexical meaning.' But what we are looking for is *cognitive meaning:* meaning that concerns the world, that says something to the effect that things are a certain way—a meaning that amounts to *thought*, in the Fregean sense of the term. The whole point of non-indexical contextualism is that by itself the sentence 'The milk is in the fridge,' does not say anything about the world, and hence has no (cognitive) meaning. It only has cognitive meaning *on a certain understanding*, one that depends on context. This is the thrust of non-indexical contextualism. It is more a matter of securing a meaning in the first place than one of altering or completing a meaning that is already there.

Of course, the lexical meaning of words plays a part in fixing cognitive meaning: in order to say something about the world we use words as we received them, that is, loaded with their '(lexical) meaning.' However, words are about the world not by virtue of their lexical meaning, but due to *the way we use them* in certain contexts. Context is not merely an addition here, it plays a pivotal role in the capacity of words—*used* words—to be about the world.

If we ponder what possible counterpart to this form of contextuality there could be at the level of the mind, we wind up with an idea that does not necessarily require the adoption of a representationalist framework—one that might even be at odds with it. This is the idea of how *fine-grained* our thoughts are, of how much more connected they are to the concrete aspects of situations than we usually take them to be. You do not think 'there is milk in the fridge' when thinking about drinking it in the same way that you do when thinking about cleaning it up. Now, the anti-contextualist fallacy consists in holding that there is a *neutral way to think this thought:* a common factor forming the basis of all the different ways of thinking the thought—an acontextual way of thinking that 'there is milk in the fridge' that is waiting to be contextualized.

We encounter several issues at this point. Firstly, if our thoughts are so fine-grained, how can it be the case that one and the same thought ever recurs? And how is the strong contextuality of every thought compatible with the fact that it seems a part of thought's definition that a particular thought can be entertained *on different occasions?*

Secondly, is it even possible to make sense of the so-called contextuality of thought, if it is to be so robust? Do we not risk reverting to the position according to which there is a fundamental *causal dependence* of thought on the world, one which makes every thought deeply dependent on the circumstances in which it is entertained? Does the claim that thoughts are so fine-grained really amount to a genuine form of *contextuality?* If so, how can that be? What is the logical structure of mental contextualism?

Thirdly, is it not still possible to make sense of indexical contextualism at the level of the mind once one has adopted an alternative framework for understanding the contextuality of mind in general? Is there no sense in saying that when I think twice, of two different sweaters, 'this is red' (supposing of course some specific circumstances), I am thinking 'the same thing' each time?

CONTEXT AND THE GENERALITY OF THOUGHT

We should first of all correct a misunderstanding regarding thought's contextuality that could result from what we have just said. It appears as though the (extremely) fine grain of many of our thoughts is not enough to make them 'contextual,' strictly speaking. After all, ontologically speaking there is nothing to prevent us from conceiving of all those thoughts—fine-grained though they might be— as acontextual entities that are grasped by the mind just as they stand. If one objects that their being so fine-grained requires an explanation, it is always possible to invoke *causality:* some thoughts might be such that very complex circumstances are required in order to produce them. This does not necessarily make such thoughts contextual, for once they have been entertained a first time it is always possible to entertain them *independently of the context* a second time. The particular situation that gave rise to them, and that perhaps is included in their content, is no longer required for the subject to entertain them. In light of this it is doubtful that it makes sense to call them 'contextual.'

On closer inspection, however, things are not so straightforward. It is true that no one can be forbidden from thinking something on a given occasion. Think whatever you like. But the grammar of thought has this essential feature: a thought can be assessed according to its *relevance*. If your thoughts are incredibly 'fine-grained' they are highly likely to quickly cross the threshold that stands between relevance and irrelevance. Precisely because of their fine grain they require that very specific conditions obtain if they are to count as being about the world (and thus, as being either true or false, as thoughts should be).

There appear to be two different strategies for dealing with *relevance*. The first consists in treating relevance as an external constraint on thought (via a *context constraint*). On this view thoughts already are thoughts, so to speak. Conditions on their being about something—and thus being true or false—only come after this fact. **However, is one really thinking something, if it is impossible to see what difference is made by what one thinks?** Would we say of someone who does not even know what it is she is thinking about, that she thinks something of a given situation? *A completely irrelevant thought just isn't a thought.* For example, I might take myself to have a thought about whether or not there is milk in the fridge, but if it turns out I do not know whether my thought ultimately concern *this* or rather *that* then I'm thinking nothing at all. I do not think anything about anything, and what I took to be a thought is, in this particular case, no thought at all.

Thus, we can treat relevance as an internal property of thoughts, of *genuine thoughts*. If what I think or take myself to think is completely irrelevant to the situation—that is, misses its fine grain—then it just isn't a thought: it claims to capture something that it cannot and as such should be interpreted as a mere appearance of a thought, something like a *mock thought*. Treating it as a thought is just to ignore to what degree particular circumstances may be part of what there is to think—not an external constraint on thoughts, but precisely their *point*. On this view, the idea of relevance amounts to the following: you cannot claim *to think something* about a certain subject if you are *missing the point*.

Understood this way, relevance constitutes a logical feature pertaining to thought's contextuality. We can call it logical because it involves a certain normative standard. It is not merely a matter of causal dependence and origin, or the occurrence of something that we might be tempted to call 'a thought.' It is precisely about whether such a thing in fact qualifies as a thought on a given occasion. Thus it concerns an essentially logical dimension pertaining to the notion of a thought: that is to say, *the possibility of being entertained on different occasions*.

This possibility just defines thought. A such, it is the central theme of contextualism, for the latter explores the circumstances under which what one takes oneself to 'think' is a genuine thought, that is to say: *a thought about a given situation*. Recently I heard a French composer make the following qualification after saying that Luc Ferrari was enjoying great success: 'The only problem is that he is dead.'

Now, *reiteratability*—the possibility of being entertained on different occasions, though perhaps not on *any* occasion—is by no means the only characteristic feature of thought. *Transposability* also appears to be distinctive of thought. Reiteratability and transposability are the two sides of what we can call thought's intrinsic *generality*. Without such generality there is nothing worthy of the name 'thought.' However, the picture becomes more complex once we consider transposability. What is the *transposition* of a thought? Intuitively, it might seem as though if a given content constitutes a thought, it is not only the case that it can be entertained on different occasions, but also that *it can be applied to different situations.* One dimension of the so-called generality of thought may well be its multi-applicability.

Now, this claim raises some significant issues. If by thought we mean a full-blooded Fregean thought, it seems the very idea of it being applied to different situations makes no sense, for *what a Fregean thought is about is part of that thought.* For if the thought is to have a definite truth-value, what the thought concerns must already be settled. From the point of view of its *aboutness*, no thought can be left indeterminate. Indeterminate contents cannot be called thoughts, at best they are fragments of—or themes for—thought.

Of course, there are different forms of aboutness. Some thoughts take very specific objects, or at least can be analysed as such. In some cases it even makes sense to talk of 'singular thoughts,' that is to say, thoughts about a single object. Reference to a particular object is part of the identity of such thoughts, of what defines them. Thus, they can recur, but only as *that very thought and about that very object.* They are entertained on different occasions, but *concerning the very same thing and in the same way.* Therefore it would not be correct to say that they are *in every sense* 'applied to different situations.' One should make a sharp grammatical distinction between *the occasion on which a thought is entertained,* and *what the thought is about.* The diversity of occasions does not amount to a diversity of objects.

However, aboutness does have a unique form. Some thoughts are about a single object. Others are about several objects or even an open-ended list of them—for example, every object that satisfies such and such condition. Even thoughts about a single object can exhibit very different kinds of generality. When I say of a certain object that 'it is red,' for example my car, this could mean that it is red 'in general' that that's the 'normal' colour of this particular object—or else that it is red *now*, at this time of the day, or perhaps in contrast to how it looked a few minutes ago before it was washed. There are many different thoughts, each about that single object, each exhibiting a different kind of generality. Some of them can be entertained at any time. Others appear to be linked to a particular point in time. This does not mean that they are purely ephemeral—prisoners of the moment that can never *be entertained on further occasions*. Nevertheless, sticking to the orthodox Fregean framework, we can say that the linguistic expression of these thoughts *will* differ on later occasions. For example, I might later say: 'at that time of day, my car looked red.'

Now, one might be tempted to think that since the linguistic expression differs—what was in the present tense is now in past tense—therefore the thought expressed cannot be the same. In fact, *it depends*. It depends precisely on *what the thought in question is about*. For some thoughts it matters that they are articulated in the present tense,[3] for others it does not. It is clear that whether or not it matters determines whether or not we are dealing with the same thought or a different one. It is a defining feature of *some kinds of thought* that they are immune to the transposition of tense that occurs in their linguistic expression. Thoughts that are not immune to such transpositions *differ* with each expression, even if they seem to retain the same content—so, in fact, their contents are *not* the same.

The question is always this: *What has been placed into a given thought* such as it has been thought on a definite occasion? What matters or not, then, for it to be counted as 'the same thought'? The identity of a thought seems to be *adaptable* to a certain degree. It depends on what one decides to let count or not, in which system one is operating. It is a bit like in classical music where it makes sense to think of a transcription of a piece of music for a new instrument as nevertheless being the same piece of music. In a musical system in which *timbre* matters more, it is no longer true that it *counts* as the same piece. Similarly, a thought is exactly that which can be *counted* as the same thought.

3. *Logical relativism*, as it is currently developing, is a way of making sense of such a view. See for instance Kölbel 2008, p. 2.

Within this framework it is possible to make better sense of a question that has once again become fashionable. As we have seen in the previous chapter, some philosophers—those that call themselves 'logical relativists'—hold that one entertains 'the same thought' when one thinks, for example, 'It is Monday' on different days, and that we should simply allow that the truth-value of this single thought varies depending on what day it is. This point of view is at odds with the Fregean orthodoxy since, from Frege's point of view, 'It is Monday' expresses a thought only if the day in question is specified, and thus there will be a different thought expressed for each different day that it refers to.

Should we part with Fregean orthodoxy by countenancing thoughts with variable truth-values? Personally I am reluctant to do this: a full-blooded thought is *a thought about the world's being some definite way*, for example, *that today is Monday*—not that 'some day' is Monday. If I treat 'today' as a variable then I have no thought. One should not confuse a template of a thought with a thought that results from filling in the template in a particular way. However, the analysis of *changes in perspective*—such as we find in narrative for instance—gives us reason to think that it makes sense to talk of the same thought being applied to different spatiotemporal locations. And after all, is it so bizarre—even in everyday life—to say that when I thought 'It's Monday' on Tuesday I entertained the same thought as I did on Monday, except that on Monday it was true and on Tuesday it was false? We certainly talk this way from time to time, and why shouldn't we?

In all these cases, the crux of the issue always comes down to what we are willing to count as *the same* thought. Without yet deciding on the difficult question of logical relativism, we can observe that when we say 'It is Monday,' in an ordinary (i.e., nonnarrative) context, it can mean two different things. On the one hand, it could be an identification of *today* as such. In which case, it does not make sense to say that the same thought could be entertained regarding another day: if it concerns another day, it is a different thought.

However, I can also think of today as something more general, its being *a* Monday, in the sense of *any* Monday—as for example when I think about something we should do on any given Monday (though not necessarily this one). In this case it no longer sounds absurd to say that I think *exactly the same* thing of this Monday or of the next one (or perhaps, by mistake, Tuesday): in such cases, the unicity of 'today' does not itself matter.

In other words, we should never forget that thought is *intentional*. If you want to know the scope of a thought you have to consider *the way in which it is thought*. This is the counterpart of linguistic contextualism in the sphere of the mental. Depending on the way in which it is thought, a thought's scope might be more or less general.

Nevertheless, it is not clear that we should ever talk of the *transposition* of thought as such, for even allowing that some kind of 'generality' pertains to the aboutness of particular thoughts, still, they are all *about exactly what they are about*. There does not appear to be any contextual flexibility here. At most we can say—if we can even say this much—that the truth-value varies; but the 'sense' does not. What could it be for 'the sense of a thought' to change, without *the thought itself changing*? In fact, what even is 'the sense of a thought'?

Making sense of transposability at the level of the mind—and of *limited transposability* as part of a contextualist position concerning that level—requires a further step: we need to *analyse thoughts*. Thoughts are, in themselves, complete. They can be entertained on different occasions, but it is not clear in which sense they can be *applied to different things*, as what they are applied to is just part of their definition. What do we mean, however, when we say that we '*think the same thing*' about different things? As we have noted, this turn of phrase seems to be an essential part of the grammar of thought. Is it not the case that thinking something entails the possibility of thinking it about another thing as well—not only *on* another occasion, but *about* another situation?

The problem seems more tractable once we observe that many thoughts, perhaps all thoughts, are *analysable*. When I think that this sweater is red, don't I think *the same thing* about it as I do about another red sweater on another occasion? From a certain point of view, the answer is 'no': the thought varies depending on which sweater is in question. In one case, it is the thought that *this* sweater is red; in the other, that *that* sweater is red. These are certainly different thoughts. From another perspective, however, one can say that both thoughts share something in common, and that on each occasion I thus think 'the same thing' about both sweaters.

This is exactly what *'concepts'* are supposed to be: things that can play the same role in different thoughts. It is essential to note that concepts, by themselves, are not thoughts. They are *pieces into which thoughts can be analysed*. This means that we can, in some extended sense of the term, be said 'to think the same thing' about two different situations. According to the standard of full-blooded thought we take there to be two different thoughts concerning two different sweaters—yet *under a certain analysis* of those thoughts we can say we think the same thing in thinking them. For instance, if I think this sweater and another sweater are both 'red,' my full-blooded thoughts concerning each of them can be considered applications of the same concept—'being red'—to an object, though a different object in each case. This is one possible analysis of these two thoughts, one that is instrumental in capturing an aspect of 'the generality of thought.'

Now, the very idea of a concept can easily lead to an anti-contextualist picture of thought: a purely compositional one according to which thoughts are composed of out of blocks that are themselves independent of any context.

However, it is possible to make room for contextuality even at this level, for, as we have said, *it does not make sense to apply just any concept in a given situation*. We have known since Frege that a concept can be represented as a function from given circumstances to truth-values. Thus, depending on the object in question, each thought in which the operation of a particular concept can be sensibly recognized is true or false. Now, what if the sweater has just been soaked with red paint or is covered in blood? Is or isn't it 'red' in the sense we previously thought it was? It seems our earlier concept of 'red' was not as universal as we might have thought, since it fails to provide us with a ready answer to this question. It is not always either *true or false* that a particular object is red *in the relevant sense of 'red.'* Thus, 'such and such is red'—on this understanding of the sense of 'red'—is not always a thought. This is not merely a problem concerning categories—though there are certainly objects to which it makes no sense to ascribe a colour—it is a problem of context: of *the particular ways in which we think something is 'red.'* (There is no way of thinking something to be, in this sense of 'way,' that is not *particular.*)

Thus, it is not the case that bringing a 'concept' into play always yields a thought. This is, however, only logical, for *thoughts, as such, are not made out of concepts.* Quite the reverse: a concept is merely the theoretical product of the way we analyse thoughts.

Of course, it is clear some concepts, like *acquired patterns of thought,* are part of the natural history of our mind and can therefore play the role of 'templates' for thought. By putting to work a concept that you already have as part of your mental equipment, you can produce a new thought—that is, if it is possible to do so by applying *this* concept, in *that* way, in *these* given circumstances. Nevertheless, the concept in question, *qua* concept, is only defined as *something that is shared by different thoughts.* Concepts only make sense against the background of the thoughts from which they are extracted through analysis.

Now, a second point we can make about concepts is that *this 'analysis' is always contextual.* From the logical perspective, Frege taught us that it is always possible to analyse a given thought in multiple ways. To take up one of his examples, the sentence: 'Cato killed himself,' expresses a thought. At least it does when used a certain way in certain circumstances. That thought can however be analysed in different ways. Either it is a particular instance of a schema according to which 'Cato killed *someone*' (that happens to be himself), or of another according to which '*someone* killed Cato,' or yet another according to which '*someone* killed *someone*,' or else in an even subtler way according to which '*someone* killed *themselves*.' These different analyses do not understand the structure of this particular thought in the same way.

Now, how should we choose between these different options in a given case? The answer is clear: it depends on *the other thoughts* we are comparing this thought to. If we have on our list: 'Cato killed Cato' and 'Catilina killed Cato,' where one is true and the other is false, it makes sense to analyse both of them as having the following structure: '. . . killed Cato.'

Of course, it might be the case that two thoughts are not enough in order for us to make a judgment concerning the structure, and that we need to enlarge the list. For only in this way can one decide *what the thought is about*, and what structure is in question crucially depends on this. For example, the thought might be about someone killing someone in general rather than someone killing Cato in particular.

The range of thoughts one compares to the thought one is analysing defines what we shall call *a context of thought*. Depending on—and only depending on—this context, one obtains a *structure*. Now, what decides which thoughts one should compare a given thought to if not the context, in the very sense that term has in the philosophy of language—the *context in which we talk and we think?*

Take for example the two analyses just envisaged. In some contexts there is no substantial difference between someone's killing someone and someone's killing themselves. This just means that in those contexts, this difference *does not matter.* So our thought can be analysed as a particular instance of the thought '*someone killed someone*' ('someone' being Cato on both sides). However, in different contexts, the thought might precisely be about killing oneself—suicide—in which case the thought that Cato killed himself should no longer be compared to the thought that Catilina killed him. They do not share the structure they were supposed to share according to the previous analysis.

The correct analysis, that is, *the conceptual breakdown of a thought*, depends on the context. Thus, if we introduce something like concepts—and we should if we want to account for the generality of thoughts—we can make sense of contextuality in the philosophy of mind in two interdependent ways:

1. As a matter of logic, we cannot apply just any concept in any context (whilst still yielding a *thought*, that is).
2. We can discern that a concept is part of a given thought only insofar as it is a genuine thought, that is to say a *thought in context*.

In light of this it is possible to say that contextualism as a thesis belongs to both the philosophy of mind and the philosophy of language. We can even say that to some degree it belongs *primarily to the philosophy of mind*. It belongs to the philosophy of language only as a consequence of the fact that language is the medium in which thought is *contextually expressed*. The contextuality of thought's expression captures something of the contextuality of thought itself. Thoughts are precisely *what are expressed contextually by different expressions*, for they are not made up of 'representations' that are immune to contextual variation. The fact that there is no absolute analysis of a given thought, but that its analysis always depends on the context is evidence of this deep contextuality. It certainly makes sense to analyse thoughts into concepts—it is part of what thought is that this analysis is possible. But concepts are not 'representations' in the atomic, acontextual sense of the term. They are not even 'representations that need to be contextualized'—as the idea of transposing *indexical contextualism* to the mental level may have seemed to suggest. Concepts grow in the spaces between different contexts.

CHAPTER NINE

Contextualizing Ontology

IF ONLY ONE THING is to be retained from the phenomenological approach to philosophy, it should be the requirement that one gives life to one's concepts, *that one fleshes them out*. As Husserl makes explicit as early as the *Logical Investigations*, the phenomenological method is, at bottom, *a method of examples*. Exemplification thus plays a major role—not as an external form of illustration or a test of some sort—but as the essential means by which concepts are determined.

Now, it might be tempting to think that the traditional concept of 'exemplification' is insufficient for accounting for the embodiment of concepts. The traditional concept of an example is plagued by the suspicion that the example is *external* to that which it supposedly exemplifies. This entails that when considering some concrete given thing as an example of something one must only retain some of its features—those that concern the concept.

One finds a striking expression of this criticism in Merleau-Ponty's *Phenomenology of Perception*:

> We can get through to the individual only by the hybrid procedure of finding an *example*, that is, by stripping it from its facticity.[1]

The *example* is thought of as the embodiment of a *type*. Thus, it is a typified individuality: an individuality in which the features that are alien to the illustrated concept are, as it were, neglected—in

1. Merleau-Ponty 1958, p. 73.

133

other words, an individual that has been stripped of its real, concrete individuality.

Merleau-Ponty's point is that there is no example that is not an example *of* some concept, and that examples are construed exclusively according to the standard set by their concept. As such, the example, *qua* example, is necessarily 'standardized,' no longer possessing the richness of the concrete phenomenon—that is, that which phenomenology should be concerned with.

One possible way of responding to this challenge consists in trying to substitute a richer, *more adequate* relation for the one traditionally described as 'exemplification.' What does 'adequate' mean here? It means that the concept, or whatever represents what is given, finds *its perfect match* in the given, that the *gap* that seems to exist between concepts and the individuals that—according to the traditional conception—serve as their examples, might be closed, and that real pieces of what is given might in fact *correspond* to the marks *(Merkmale)* included in the representation.

During the last few decades Analytic metaphysics has (re)introduced this idea under the title of *instantiation* as opposed to mere exemplification.[2] Indeed, instantiation is supposed to be a more intimate relation than exemplification has traditionally been conceived of as being. One can make this point by adopting the language of 'truth-makers.' If *a* is an example of the concept *F*, *Fa* is true, but we do not know why *Fa* is true—that is, what it is about *a* that makes *F* true of it. So the relation between *F* and its 'example' appears to provide a mapping that is structurally *coarse-grained*. The relation of *instantiation*, on the other hand, is intended to map what is given in an essentially *fine-grained* way. It might be described thus: There is a realized relation of instantiation if *a* has a feature f_a that embodies F—that is a *particular and real instance of F*: f_a is *what makes F true of a*. As such, to some extent, one might be

2. See, for example, Bacon 2011.

tempted to say that the true basis of exemplification lies in instantiation. Some 'contact' has been found here between representation and real presence (i.e., something really given) that grounds the capacity of a representation to be a 'representation of' what it represents. One might call this kind of 'contact' 'adequate fulfilment.'

From this perspective phenomenology, or at least a certain kind of phenomenology, is able to play a part here. If we go back to Husserl's early metaphysical investigations, we shall certainly find something along these lines. One significant connection is that the early Husserl makes room in his ontology for *abstract particulars* ('moments' in his terminology)—which also seem to be a basic requirement in the story we have just told. Of course, Husserl was not the only author to have such entities in his ontological inventory, even in his own time.[3] Indeed, phenomenology has no monopoly on the ontological thesis in question—one could endorse it without having any kind of commitment to phenomenology. It is true however that it plays an important role in the phenomenological perspective, insofar as it is primarily concerned with giving an account of what is given in all its concreteness. What is 'given' is not merely a pole of predication: some general object 'X' in all its formality; it is a concrete individual with real, particular features.

Let us admit that an ontology of abstract particulars (of real *'properties'*) seems to be a particularly convenient one for phenomenology, because it allows a grip on the subtle concrete aspects of things as they appear. However, on the basis of this ontology we must go beyond the merely generic demand for examples and take a further step by seeking a more intimate relation between our concepts and what is given (the particular *aspects* of what is given): that of instantiation.

Now, I am extremely sceptical about such a perspective. To my mind, attempting to overcome the device of mere exemplification by adopting an alleged mirroring relation between our concepts and

3. On the other side of the Channel one might think, for example, of Cook Wilson.

'what is given' cuts thought off from the world rather than bringing us closer to it, for it leads us to a view that ignores the inherent richness and complexity of the relation of exemplification. We should amend an insufficient analysis of exemplification by investigating its concrete conditions, not by replacing it with an allegedly transparent relation that is independent of any *contextual frame*.

To see the problem let us take a closer look at the early Husserl investigation into the logic and ontology of abstraction. In a preparatory manuscript (ended in 1893) for his *Psychological Studies in the Elements of Logic* (published in 1894), Husserl makes a very important distinction:

> Concepts must, I would like to believe, absolutely not be identified with abstract presentations *(abstracte Vorstellungen).*[4]

Husserl's reason is that it is misleading to call concepts 'presentations' *(Vorstellungen)*, for presenting only makes sense if some kind of *presence* is involved. To present is just to *make something present*.

Now, "to have a content present—of whatever nature, whether abstract or concrete—does not yet mean to have a concept."[5] Bare presence, by itself, is not conceptual. "We first have a concept where with a certain content (. . .) certain further dispositions are linked, in virtue of which it can accomplish all of that which the concept accomplishes for us in knowledge."[6]

We can ignore the part about dispositions, which stems from Herbart, and belongs to Husserl's very early naturalistic approach in which he tended to base intentionality on a kind of psychic economy. (This framework was overcome at the end of 1893 in his tentative reflections toward a continuation of the first published part of the

4. Edmund Husserl, "Intuition and Repräsentation, Intention and Fulfilment" (Husserl 1979, pp. 269–302), in Husserl 1994, p. 328. I substitute 'presentations' for 'representations' in Dallas Willard's translation—it makes better sense given Husserl's emphasis on *presence*.

5. Husserl 1994, pp. 328–329.

6. Husserl 1994, p. 329.

Psychological Studies in the Elements of Logic.) This leaves us with the point that a concept is not a mere intuition, and therefore not a mere presence either: some sort of *surplus* is required in order to make sense of it as a concept. There is a concept, in other words, only where the intuitively given is considered from a certain angle. Consequently, concepts are not characterized so much by abstraction as they are by a kind of cognitive take on what is given—a *perspective* on the latter, one might say.

That said, there seems to be another side to the story. If *abstraction* doesn't have to do with concepts, then *what is it?* And, if it has to do with something other than concepts, what is the relation between concepts and these abstract entities that are *not* concepts? Husserl, following in the footsteps of some other Brentanists like Carl Stump, makes the brilliant move of introducing abstraction *into the heart of intuition, into presence as such.* We can be presented with either concrete or abstract contents. This results in a formal theory of concrete and abstract contents, as expounded in the first of the *Studies* published in 1894—a theory whose basis is psychological, but the import of which is clearly ontological.

Now, what are 'abstract contents'? They certainly needn't be 'general.' They can merely be parts of what is given, particular aspects of what is intuited. Today Husserl is constantly saluted, deservingly so, as one of those who, on the cusp of twentieth-century philosophy, discovered the so-called 'particular abstracts,' thereby significantly expanding the world's stock of ontological furniture. (Or perhaps we should say 'rediscovered,' given that there was already something of the sort in the scholastic tradition.) As Husserl is a Brentanist, there is certainly some truth in this.

Now, what is an 'abstract content'? It is, for example, the blackness of the ink that is in *this* bottle on my desktop, *this blackness as seen at some definite moment.* It is abstract precisely because this blackness, whether we consider it psychologically or ontologically,[7]

7. This is the story of the transition from the *Studies* of 1894 to the IIIrd *Logical Investigation,* (see IIIrd *Logical Investigation,* §§5–7) and from Stumpf's psychological per-

is not an independent object but appears or *is* only insofar as it is dependent on another object. This blackness is essentially the blackness *of this bottle at such and such a time*, and therefore only exists 'on the condition that' the bottle exists—as 'part' of the bottle. It does not seem, at least on Husserl's analysis, that the converse is true: the ink bottle does not require the blackness in order to exist (it might have been red or transparent). This bottle is an 'independent object' whereas its blackness is a dependent object—an object dependent on the independent object that the bottle is. Of course, in some deep sense, the notion of 'independence' can only be relative: all objects are, in some sense, dependent on the world.

Now, how are concepts related to the ontological structure in which what is given has parts or aspects that might themselves in turn be given (an 'abstract' given requiring a further intuitive act as its proper basis)? The draft for the *Study* suggests a very interesting answer. What happens wherever the concept 'is functioning'?

> We have a certain concretum, absolute or relative, which we consider exclusively with respect to its possession of certain partial contents. This involves our attending to these parts primarily, and relating them to the whole, thus also attending primarily to the abstract *relation* of the parts to the whole. In this we position ourselves at the 'standpoint' of the whole, so that it becomes the subject term which bears in itself, as a property, the having of the predicate terms: a 'having' specifically determined by the type of the parts.[8]

In this beautiful passage, Husserl outlines a kind of *mereological origin of predication*. It is in selecting a part in contrast to the whole to which it belongs that we find some kind of intuitive counterpart to, and origin of, a predicate.

The point, however, is that something more is required for the selected property to take on the value of a 'predicate' proper; that is to say in some sense the subject should become 'empty,' should be

---

spective on dependence and independence to Husserl's ultimate *ontological* perspective on the same issue.

8. Husserl 1994, p. 329.

seen as 'any' subject, something Husserl calls "an indifferent point of reference." Thus,

It is no [longer] 'this-here' for us, but is rather a 'something.'[9]

This emptying of the subject is an absolute condition for making the property a *concept*. The point being that, as a concept, it might constitutively be the property of *any* subject—one aspect of what Gareth Evans would call the "constraint of generality," as a general characterization of the conceptual.

The result is that, *qua* concept, the property can no longer be a *real part* of the object, but is only a kind of *formal part*, something which *might* belong to another object. It remains the fact that, in Husserl's view, there is a strict *correspondence* between, on one side, the concept as such—which is no longer a 'particular' since its being a concept means it might belong to *any* object—and on the other side, the real parts of particular things to which that concept correctly applies.

This is something that comes out clearly in subsection 7 of the very same draft. There Husserl asks how it is possible to obtain "authentic understanding" *(eigentliches Verständnis)* of a conceptual representation. In his view, it consists in acquiring "the intuition intended by the latter"[10] (not "the intuition of what it intends," as Willard's translation has it). Thus the idea, as Husserl presents it, is that any "conceptual representation" basically intends an *intuitive presentation*. In order to make full sense of the concept we just need to grasp the corresponding intuitive presentation.

In the background of this early developmental stage of Husserl's thought lies a genetic hypothesis that relies on an *abstractionist* model. Typically, according to Husserl, our conceptual representation was initially "accompanied by intuition." Thus, we are intending something that we have already experienced as 'given.' On the other hand, according to this view, what is basic about concepts

9. Husserl 1994, p. 329.
10. Husserl 1979, p. 299. See Willard's translation in Husserl 1994, p. 342.

is that *it is possible to use them in order to represent something that has not yet been given*. How can this be the case?

Here Husserl seemingly advances a kind of compositionality hypothesis. He gives the following example:

> In order to represent a red inkstand, of which I at the moment have no intuition, there by chance serves me for the abstraction of the colour the red writing pad at hand, and, for the abstraction of the external form, the black inkstand nearby.[11]

Thus, in order to present myself with something that is not given but only conceptually represented, and to confer some intuitive givenness on that thing, I pick up particular features of the things around me that are intuitively given and intuitively compose the figure of the merely represented thing, in effect *constructing* a tailor-made intuitive counterpart to my conceptual representation. The question, of course, concerns the *unifying power* that puts both pieces of givenness together despite the fact they are "objectively *(sachlich)* separated." At this early stage of his thought Husserl calls it "interest" *(Interesse)*—a coinage he will harshly criticize later on.

The striking part of this story is that Husserl describes the 'transference' of so-called particular abstracts in such a way that he clearly occupies the corner of contemporary trope-theory inhabited by those who believe in the possibility of *transferable* 'tropes.'

> Then the redness seems to break loose *(sich loszulösen)* from the pad, to wander over to the inkstand and suffuse it.[12]

Thus, it appears to be possible to detach that particular piece of actual redness—the redness of the pad—such that it is subsequently available for possible recombination. Now the inkstand (given in imagination) possesses the pad's redness. But this is still the pad's redness and no other redness, especially not any "redness in general."

11. Husserl 1994, p. 342.
12. Husserl 1994, p. 342.

However, Husserl makes an important qualification:

The redness does not actually break loose (*die Röte löst sich nicht wirklich los*). Rather, an indeterminately delimited (vacillating, blurry) bit of the surface which bears it does.[13]

"Redness" is such an abstract moment that it is impossible to maintain any intuitive meaning for it if it does not accompany the intuition of some kind of surface of which it is the redness. What happens, and what must happen for there to be a real transference of the "trope" *as such*, is that the intuition of its bearer becomes partly "blurred." It is necessary for some part of the intuitive givenness to become "indeterminate" in order to make the other part a mere piece of transferable givenness. However, the surface of the inkstand which the specific property of the pad's redness now adheres to is not at all blurry. Although not the pad's, it is a perfectly determinate surface. There is nothing blurry about it.

Why this story about blurriness? What does it *correspond* to? *It corresponds throughout the account to what precisely cannot be dealt with in terms of 'correspondence.'*

Why should we render the outline of the coloured surface mentally 'blurry' in order to make the phenomenological feature that is the particular colour applicable to another object, to another bearer of properties? This bearer of properties is, as it were, 'left blank' insofar as we consider the property as belonging to one or another object to which the concept: 'being coloured in exactly this way' may be applied. Thus, this element of the story is connected to the fact that at this point abstract particulars are still considered possible illustrations of *concepts*, and as such provide an ontological-psychological answer to the difficult question of the embodiment of concepts—a better answer than that supplied by the mere notion of exemplification, which seemingly remains groundless.

Now, my point here is that, as interesting as the ontological story about abstract particulars might be, it cannot do the job it is supposed

13. Husserl 1994, p. 342.

to do—that of grounding concepts by providing them with a phenom-enological basis. For nothing can spare us the *effort* of *applying* the concepts we have, an effort that involves normative assessment that can never be understood in terms of a mere 'match.'

Let us consider the case of the black ink in the inkstand.[14] We fill a fountain pen with ink from the inkstand and write something with it. The writing is blue. Is the ink 'blue' or 'black'? Well, it *depends* on how the question is meant: on whether 'being black' means 'being black in the bottle' or 'being black on the page.' In the first case, the ink in the bottle is black; in the second case, it is not. However, it would be a mistake to think that there must be *two different concepts* of 'black' at work here. It is part of the *flexibility* of our concept of 'black' that it might apply, on one understanding, to the ink in the bottle or, on another understanding, to how the ink looks on the page. The concept 'black' can represent either of these things.

Now, it would be extremely misleading to say that in both cases there is the same chunk of reality (the same blackness) that, in one instance, appears in the liquid in the bottle and, in another instance, in the writing on the paper—and furthermore that *their different ways of being black simply consist in their having this common feature.* As though by virtue of possessing this common feature both counted as being *black in the very same sense.* They are not. It might indeed turn out that there is a common ontological feature, an 'entity,' present in both situations. But the question is whether the presence of such an entity is *relevant.* After all, it might exist (granting for the sake of argument there are such entities) without rendering the corresponding concept at all 'adequate.' Since the concept 'by itself' is nothing, what matters is *how it is meant.* The particular abstract blackness (i.e., the blackness of the ink in the bottle) may exist in cases where the corresponding concept of blackness is irrelevant. This is true when, for example, I ask 'is that ink black?'

14. I take this example from Charles Travis (see among others Travis 2000) who inspired my critical analysis of the metaphysics of properties.

where what I want to know is if it writes black—a perfectly accept-able understanding of what ink being 'black' amounts to.

As such, the problem that lies in the vicinity of concepts is not so much their match in givenness, but rather the way in which they *connect* to their match; the way in which they define something as counting, or failing to count, *as* their match. If one reasons concep-tually then the problem is inescapable. That is to say, there is no way to preserve the advantage gained by reasoning with concepts—of acknowledging their right—whilst simultaneously reducing them to *a decontextualized image of a piece of something present.* In other words, no concepts exist independently of their *uses,* or of all the normativity that essentially pertains to those uses. Any at-tempt to derive concepts merely from the alleged naturalness of the way things are (e.g., the naturalness of what is given) is doomed to failure.

The problem concerning concepts, as Frege formulated so clearly, essentially concerns what 'being true of' consists in. Even when as-sessments of truth are immediate, and in some sense 'evident,' some norm is still always involved. The task is not merely one of gath-ering up pieces of what is given, but of assessing them according to a 'standard.'

For example, consider *general* concepts. (Here we broach a very different problem from the one which we have dealt with thus far. It is not anymore about *the intrinsic generality of concepts*—this dif-ference must be emphasized if we are to avoid a certain widespread confusion.) One might try to reduce a general concept to the mere *similarity* of abstract particulars that belong to each object in the domain of the general concept in question—a strategy explicitly de-nounced by Husserl in his II^d *Logical Investigation*. Thus, whereas the hair of my Japanese friends in the audience in front of me is all 'black' in some generic (and so no longer particular) sense of the term, present in each person's hair are different abstract particulars that are *similar* to one another—as opposed to *the same* abstract particular being present only in each person's hair.

Founding the sense of a concept in a *similarity* between the objects in its domain probably makes good phenomenological sense. However, insofar as what is at stake is our being justified in applying a specific concept, what matters is not just similarity, but the particular *normative* status of that similarity, that is, whether it is *sufficient*. If two objects fall under the same concept, that means they in some way belong to the same 'type.' Now, the concept of a type is not a natural concept, that is, devoid of normativity. As Austin puts it:

'Is of a type with which' means 'is sufficiently like those standard states of affairs with which.' Thus, for a statement to be true one state of affairs must be like certain others, which is a natural relation, but also *sufficiently* like to merit the same 'description,' which is no longer a purely natural relation. To say 'This is red' is not the same as to say 'This is like those,' nor even as to say 'This is like those which were called red.' That things are similar, or even 'exactly' similar, I may literally see, but that they are *the same* I cannot literally see—in calling them the same colour a convention is involved additional to the conventional choice of the name to be given to the colour which they are said to be.[15]

As we are working at the level of concepts and not at the level of language (even if the study of expression should play a leading role in disclosing the variety of ways in which we may state—and so think—things to be) we can drop the presupposition concerning the allegedly universal *conventional* basis of normativity. Language is certainly conventional. It is unclear, however, whether it makes sense to call *thought* conventional. Nevertheless, what emerges from Austin's analysis is the idea that thought is *normative*. A concept is a normative structure. Thus, it does not simply match a given similarity or a natural fact. It *measures* them. As such the paradoxes that are usually put forward as revealing the intrinsic boundaries of concepts (at what point does the addition of a grain of sand result in a heap?) on the contrary reveal a positive aspect of them. Conceptual

15. From chapter 5, "Truth," in Austin 1961, p. 122.

thinking is concerned precisely with making normative decisions about cases in which a concept applies and cases in which it does not. Defining a range of application is not something external to a concept. It is part of what a concept—as well as 'conceptual' reasoning—is. This is exactly what the idea of 'doing without concepts' misses: the *measurement* of what is given.

One might therefore say that the epistemology of trope-theorists is prone to becoming the naturalistic epistemology of *gatherers*, whereas the friends of concepts should rather adopt an epistemology of *farmers*. The latter focus on organizing rather than merely collecting the given—on constructing a normative framework according to which the given can be assessed and drawn upon. This point is not restricted to the 'general concepts' we have just considered. It is an absolutely general point about concepts as such, even *ones that are not general* in this particular sense of the term (that is, as opposed to so-called 'particular' or even 'singular' concepts).

In fact, we can certainly grant Gareth Evans and John McDowell the point that there are *singular concepts*—for it is possible to think of a particular object *as the object it is* in all its singularity. However even 'singular' concepts constitute a standard that may or may not be correctly applied to a given thing—this is exactly what is in question in cases of reidentification or re-characterization. A concept needn't be 'general' in the sense of 'being applicable to *different objects*.' However, it does need to be general in another, absolutely essential sense, that of *being applicable on different occasions* (this is the real significance of the 'constraint of generality').

Through my concept of 'John' I always think about the same person. But it is essential that I can do it on different occasions—that I can claim to reidentify John as John (even if sometimes I am mistaken, and mistake Peter for 'John'). Furthermore, it is essential that I can successively characterize John as a nice man, a coward, and so on—taking for granted all the while that he is the same John and that I *understand* through the concept 'John' the same John.

This is the other aspect of Evans's 'constraint of generality,' which is as valid for singular concepts as it is for 'general' ones. Both parts of Evans's formulation are equally important:

1) An F should be such that if Fa is possible, Fb, etc., is also possible.

But also:

2) An a should be such that if Fa is possible, Ga, etc., is also possible.

In Evans's combined formulation:

If $Fa \wedge Gb$, then $Ga \wedge Fb$ should be possible.

From our perspective what should be emphasized is that the recognition that the a that is G is the very same a that is F is just as *normative* as the recognition that the two red samples are both 'red.' Austin's point remains as true of numerical identity as it does of descriptive identity: 'That things are similar, or even 'exactly' similar, I may literally see, but that they are *the same* I cannot literally see.' Identity is not a merely 'natural property.' Insofar as it makes sense only in contrast to a possible *nonidentity*, it is essentially normative. Thus, it makes room for some assessment, or measure of, what *counts as being the same.*

Have we not returned to precisely the logic we were trying to escape, in which concepts are constituted by *abstractions?* Where concepts—even individual ones (if there are any)—are standards applied to what is given *from outside?* It depends on what conception of the generality constraint we endorse.

It is very difficult to purge concepts of all generality in the precise sense of 'generality' we have just seen. There is a concept only where there is *a way of referring* that is somehow *available* for thought and that can be reactivated across different occasions. This does not mean that that 'generality' could ever, or should ever, be *absolute*— something that Evans's formal wording of the constraint might suggest. This idea lacks phenomenological sense. Concepts do not provide us with a formal framework that can be applied to what is given from without, independently of *how what is given is given to us*, or of the particular kinds of given thing we happen to be dealing with. As such, the question of the 'fittingness' of our concepts to what is given is a genuine one. 'Generality' cannot mean: 'independence' from things as they are given. The example of 'singular concepts' whose constitution is, as a rule, *object-dependent*, proves that the opposite is true.

One must be careful, however, not to misapply the *phenomenological constraint*. This constraint—on a par with the 'generality constraint'—does not apply to the referent (which just is what it is), at least not *directly*. There is nothing intrinsically phenomenological about a mere theory of the referent: no ontology is *by itself* phenomenological. The phenomenological constraint, insofar as it is logical, is placed on *meaning*. As far as concepts are concerned a phenomenological theory of meaning is a phenomenological determination of concepts, that, as such, *depends to some extent on the given to which concepts determine themselves as being applicable.*

What is phenomenological in all this is that it is *constitutive* of concepts that there are some particular occasions that are considered to be *cases to which they typically apply*. The circularity here is decisive: the fact that the occasion is considered 'typical' means that *it is already assessed according to the standard of the concept.* Conversely, the particular application is required for defining the type: the type of thing in question is that which is 'of the same type as . . .'

As such, there is a precedence accorded to givenness—something traditionally thought to characterize the phenomenological stance in philosophy—that at the same time does not dismiss the role that concepts play in our relation to the given. This does not mean that it is possible, in accordance with some fantasy of a 'perfect match,' to find a shadow of our concepts in the given itself—a requirement not so much impossible to meet as it is *senseless*, given what concepts are. It simply means that our concepts always depend on the given in an essential way. They are the concepts adopted by beings that exist in a determinate world (in *the* world), and in many determinate ways. Thus, we should *put our conceptualizations back into the world*. This is far better than trying to take a shortcut to the world that avoids concepts, and then later pretending to reconnect them to what we have allegedly managed to thereby reach.

Now, from this point of view, exemplification seems to do much better than the relation of instantiation, for it allows one to incorporate, as an essential part of the story about what concepts are, *the 'backwards effect' concepts have on themselves in being applied.*

Paradoxically what is both helpful and necessary here is the *gap* that always exists between a concept and its *examples*—the very gap that friends of instantiation strive so desperately to close. This gap can be, as it were, projected onto the given itself, by making a piece of what is given *serve as a standard for other pieces of what is given*. That is, by allowing pieces of what is given to be compared to one another not only insofar as they are similar, but insofar as they are *different*. The idea is no longer one of founding the normative (i.e., concepts) in the natural (i.e., abstract chunks of reality), but of *making the experience of the natural itself normative*, insofar as it is drawn upon in the concrete elaboration of concepts.

We can turn once more to Merleau-Ponty in order to make sense of this. We saw earlier that Merleau-Ponty harshly criticizes examples for being merely external illustrations of concepts that, by themselves, are alien to the given and so unable to capture it in its concreteness. Concrete *experiences are not, by themselves, examples*—that is his point, and there is certainly some truth in it.

However in another passage concrete intuitive experience (still understood in contrast to the 'general type') *becomes its own example:*

> When I contemplate an object with the sole intention of watching it exist and unfold its riches before my eyes, then it ceases to be an allusion to a general type, and I become aware that each perception, and not merely that of sights which I am discovering for the first time, re-enacts on its own account the birth of intelligence and has some element of creative genius about it: in order that I may recognize the tree as a tree, it is necessary that, beneath this familiar

meaning, the momentary arrangement of the visible scene should begin all over again, as on the very first day of the vegetable kingdom, to outline the individual idea of this tree.[16]

What Merleau-Ponty contests is the philosophical and psychological fallacy according to which the type is pre-constituted, setting an *external* norm for the perceptual experience itself. Of course, the type usually *is* pre-constituted, but as long as we're focusing on *perception* as such (on 'what we see,' as Austin would say), it is wrong to say that the perceptual type is pre-constituted—that is, constituted before perception. Now, Merleau-Ponty does not quite say that in perception there are no types: in perception we find, or more precisely *sketch*, 'the individual idea of this tree.' And the recognition of this tree *as a tree* depends on this basic ability to see it as '*this* tree,' and thus 'outline' *(dessiner)* this individual idea concretely. It is as if each experience of a tree were already *the sketch of something*, a kind of schematization. So our ability to recognize something as a tree, and thus possess the 'concept' of tree, depends on our basic capacity to see this thing here as *this tree*, that thing over there as *that tree*, and so on.

This does not mean that we should return to an abstractionist model according to which the 'general' concept of tree is a kind of logical *residue* obtained by abstraction from the 'individual ideas' of the different trees. It just means that our capacity to categorize anything as a tree is directly dependent on our capacity to treat some particular cases as *paradigm cases* of what a tree is: it is in this precise sense that they are 'ideas' (individual ideas, but ideas nonetheless) and not merely pieces of 'experience.' In experiencing them, we take them to in some way constitute a standard.

'Individual ideas' are *that on which conceptualization draws and depends*—not just that *to* which conceptualization is applied from outside. It is *the name of the given insofar as it may itself be made into a normative standard*. But, if it is made into a normative standard, it is decisive not only that a tree might be similar to another tree, but that it might be similar to it while also being different.

16. Merleau-Ponty 1958, pp. 50–51.

Indeed, even *insofar as it is different:* the fact that one tree outlines the shape of what being *a tree* amounts to is an invitation for another tree to do so *differently*—for different ways of being realized may be necessary in order for 'the same' thing to be realized.

From this perspective the logic of exemplification is far more interesting than the logic of instantiation, precisely because, adequately reinterpreted, it allows us to make sense of the *gap* between the model and that of which it is a model, whether in terms of their similarity or their dissimilarity.

Let us consider an example that will allow us to both clarify the distinction between exemplification and instantiation as well as the advantages the logic of exemplification brings in contrast to instantiation: the concept of *courage.* One might think Hector, who by confronting Achilles faces certain death, is an example of courage. One might also say that in a (different?) sense Andromache—who accepts and suffers Hector's departure, keeping her strength to protect their son—is another. Now, a friend of instantiation would say that, in Hector, there is an abstract particular (a particular moral property) that is an *instance of courage,* and that, in Andromache there is another abstract particular that is another *instance of courage.* Of course, the abstract particular that makes Hector courageous (let us call it Hector's bravery) is not the same as the abstract particular that makes Andromache courageous (let's call it Andromache's bravery). However, both of them are instances of courage, for both of them are a particular embodiment of the very same thing: courage.

Some people may find this style of analysis reassuring, for it purports to provide an *ontological embodiment* of things, like 'courage,' that we may otherwise feel quite uncertain about. Nevertheless, it may turn out that this solution merely avoids the real difficulty. For the problem is not just that Andromache's bravery and Hector's bravery are numerically different (this is the *false problem* of abstraction disguised as an ontological issue). The real problem is that it might turn out that *being courageous in Andromache's case and being courageous in Hector's case are not the same thing*—which does nothing to diminish the fact that both are genuinely courageous. They are not courageous in 'the same way.' The mistake consists in identifying the diverse ways of being courageous with as many *entities*. It is clear that Hector and Andromache are ontologically different. It is also clear that the fact that the very same notion of courage applies to them in different ways has something to do with their differing ontologically. However, it is utterly mistaken to think that for each of them there exists a *specific* entity, the force of which alone makes each count as courageous in their own way—as if the very same entity could, if transferred to the other (if this is even possible), make them courageous in that way. If Hector said, 'I shall wait for you at home and take care of our son,' he would probably pass for a coward according to the values of the Greek epic—and yet that is precisely what, by the same system of values, qualifies Andromache as a courageous woman, a *paradigm of courage*, even. This comparison might seem crude, but we can introduce more subtlety by pointing out that the same attitude that makes Andromache a courageous woman would not, in different (let us say more ordinary) circumstances, make another woman courageous. There is nothing in itself heroic about waiting for one's man at home—unless you know that he is never coming back and you do so with a certain 'nobility of mind,' a quality that is very difficult to describe other than through examples like Andromache's.

In other words, the point is not that it is possible to find instances that fall under the same concept that are very different (not just numerically, but qualitatively) yet that still answer to the same meaning. It is more that the same concept can be applied to things in very different ways that are not as such transferable—that might highlight either very different aspects of the things in question or very similar aspects, but perhaps *for very different reasons*. An x being *F* is not always the same thing, and this is essential to the determination of the concept *F*. For instance, *our* concept of courage feeds on the examples of Hector *and* Andromache. We would not have the same conception of courage if we were not able to apply it to Andromache.

The idea of exemplification is far better than that of instantiation when it comes to representing this fact, for it does not rely on the idea of finding a match for some property that we have a prior grasp of. On the contrary, it makes room for the possibility of quite different things being, in their difference, examples of the same concept. What on a superficial understanding might be regarded as the weakness of examples—that is to say their ostensible looseness—is in fact their strength. If examples seem epistemologically 'loose' then it is probably because we can have the impression of not ultimately knowing *why a* is an example of *F*. Hence the temptation to find in *a* something to which *F* 'really applies' (some alleged F_a). However, this is an absurd strategy: what F 'really applies' to is just what F adequately characterizes, what fits it—that is to say: *that which is F*. Now, in this case, *a* is F. F_a, if anything like that exists, is not itself F—it would make no sense to say that such an entity is *F*. Now if what F really applies to is just *what is F*, we must recall that there are *many ways for something to be F*. Exploring the concept of F further means making a concrete investigation into these various different ways by exploring what kind of givenness and what relation to givenness they each involve. What therefore matters are not *bare pieces of givenness* of which it is impossible to form a concept (for concepts never apply to such things.) What matters is *real, full-blooded givenness*, for example Hector or Andromache in all their respective determinacy. It is very difficult to say in each case *why* one or the other of them is 'courageous'; but the fact that both might be thought of as 'courageous' is certainly *a determining factor in our concept of courage*—something that allows us to think of other characters as courageous or otherwise, and that constitutes a concrete normative standard for such assessment. Examples constitute such norms because they provide *models of application*, as opposed to bare instances of a concept (if such things even exist). They provide the opportunity to see not only that to which the concept is applied, but also *the way* or *ways* in which it can be applied.

In other words, examples reflect, in all their concreteness—for real examples are *concrete;* they are not abstract particulars—the various ways that *an intentional life clears a path through things.* This is something that cannot be reduced to chunks of things—whether mental or physical—silently mirroring each other. Thus, what is needed is an ontology that never forgets how what we apply our concepts to, as well as the particular ways in which we apply them, matters *to* those concepts. In which case, the question of what it is to be an *F* proves inseparable from the fact that *we already take some a*s *or b*s *to be* F *in particular ways.* We might call this way of addressing the ontological question of what there is—*of what we would say exists in particular circumstances—sensitive ontology.*

CHAPTER TEN

Ontology without Context

PLATONISM has been such a central issue in the philosophy of mathematics, that it has sometimes seemed to have been its *sole* concern. Philosophers tend to keep asking whether or not mathematical objects exist, and in such an abstract fashion that it is often very difficult to know whether the question makes any sense. It is as though the ontological decision regarding mathematics lay *beyond mathematics* itself and belonged to a purely metaphysical discussion. On the other hand, Platonism, in what is likely a different meaning of the word, appears to be *the default belief* of the working mathematician. This undoubtedly makes sense: How can you work on entities if you think they don't exist?

However, we should note firstly that it is not obvious that mathematics always consists in working on *entities*. One should inquire into the particular conditions under which mathematical practice can be described in this way. It may be the case that some parts of mathematics answer that description, others not. 'Mathematical objects' as such may only form *a part* of what mathematics is concerned with. Of course, if that is true the philosopher should still take into account that aspect of mathematics, whilst at the same time paying attention to the mathematician's own picture of her activity.

We should note secondly that if Platonism is a matter of taking some particular entities to exist, the question unavoidably arises as to what, in this case, it means 'to exist.' After all, if it is simply a matter of *positing* some entities and affirming that 'they are'—or,

more precisely, that 'there is / are some entity / entities such that
. . .'—as we constantly do in mathematics, for example, in the result
of a proof of existence—it is very doubtful that this entails any real
kind of 'Platonism.' The word 'Platonism' seems to imply a more
substantial ontological commitment.

One can put the point more technically by saying that Platonism
consists in the belief that the entities in question exist *beyond and
independently of the proof of their existence*. With this we enter the
logical space of the traditional Platonism debate. It is common in
this debate to draw a contrast between *invention* and *discovery*. *Er-
finden* versus *entdecken*, as Friedrich Waismann puts it in his *Introduction to mathematical thinking*,[1] to cite just one example. On
the one hand, one *invents* what could not have existed independently of having been invented. On the other hand, one *discovers*
what is *already there* to be discovered.

What makes the whole debate so tricky is that there is something fishy about the dichotomy. Until now it appears that Platonism has won all its victories by guilt-tripping its opponents. Platonists usually try to convince us that if we do not buy into their
allegedly transcendent entities, then we shall fall prey to some kind
of *fictionalism: either* the mathematical entities, whatever they
might be, are transcendent, *or* they are *fictitious.* The second horn of
the dilemma renders mathematical entities so subjective and arbi-
trary that it seems as though they could just be *anything.* Since we
wish to avoid this consequence, we are forced to accept Platonism.

Indeed, there is probably something mistaken in the very application of the notion of 'invention' to mathematical entities; it
suggests that we created them independently of any structural
constraint—that *we made them up.* The fully-fledged fictionalist
interpretation of mathematics is certainly difficult to stomach. It is
at odds with the strong *sense of objectivity* experienced by the
working mathematician.

1. Waismann [1936] 1996.

However, I do not see why the collapse of the strongly construc-tivist model should compel us to accept the opposing model, that of *naïve discovery*. The complex shape of a tree's leaves can clearly be described using mathematical objects; nevertheless, mathematical objects do not grow on trees. They are not *'naturally given.'* Now, one way of formulating the question of Platonism is to ask whether that which is not 'naturally given' can be *'given'* at all. This is not to say that some objects are 'too good' to be given, and so remain be-yond the scope of givenness. The point is that 'being given' just *is* 'being naturally given' (somehow or other, whether perceptually or otherwise)—that is, is something encountered as what it is *indepen-dently of what we do*. From this perspective, Platonism can be thought of as a *naturalistic* model of mathematics, one character-ized by the fact that it approaches the mathematical realm as though it were *a form of natural realm*.

Thus far, it appears that the discussion surrounding Platonism has excessively—almost exclusively—focused on the ontology of this 'natural' realm. The commonsense view has difficulty ac-cepting what it thinks of as a kind of hyper-nature, one that differs from that which common sense is acquainted. On the other hand, mathematical Platonists insist that, in addition to that familiar sort of nature, mathematicians are genuinely acquainted with nonphys-ical objects in a way that is more or less analogous to that in which ordinary people are acquainted with sensible objects. Of course, the whole point of the controversy is that this form of acquaintance is both *the same and not the same* as the ordinary kind. Mathematical objects are not perceived—as people commonly say: the mathemat-ical circle is *not seen*—yet it is *as if* the mathematician perceived these objects in all their transcendent being. Mathematical Pla-tonism feeds on the tacit analogy with ordinary perception, though at the same time it supposedly transcends ordinary perception.

Now, in my view, the problem here is not the idea of a hyperphys-ical (i.e., nonphysical) nature, but the very idea of *nature*. The meta-phor of discovery that is connected to the idea of nature is extremely misleading. Of course, this is not to deny that there are any *discoveries* in mathematics, or that such discoveries at times take the specific form of discovering objects. To reiterate, philosophy should certainly take into account this essential dimension of the mathematician's experience.

However, the discoveries made by the working mathematician *only make sense within a mathematical context.* If there is an ontology to be found in mathematics—that is, *within the mathematical framework*—it is not the ontology of hunter-gatherers roaming the jungle, but of farmers who have staked out their fields. Is mathematics not entirely a matter of 'harvest and sowing,' in Alexander Grothendieck's words? This does not mean that one never happens to find a rock in one's field, or that no quarrels over boundaries ever break out. It just means that 'discoveries' are only possible *in an already mathematized universe.* They are not *mere encounters* with a naked exteriority.

Now, the problem with mathematical Platonism is that it tends to make mathematical objectivity so strong as to place it *beyond* mathematics, so to speak—as though mathematical entities had a being of their own independently of *their life in mathematics.* Jean-Yves Girard's sarcastic remark, in which he derides our naive picture of the set of integers as an infinite showroom of hunting trophies, makes a lot of sense.[2] If we are going to tackle the issue of mathematical objectivity, we should observe it *in the place it works*—and see *how* it works there—as opposed to where it ends up once it's been stuffed and deprived of life, as it were.

But my point is not about mathematical Platonism as such. For once its metaphysical interpretation has been destabilized the question of its truth might turn out to be a local one which retains its legitimacy *within* a mathematical framework. As a philosopher, what matters to me is rather that, in fact, some interpretation of mathematical Platonism serves as *a general standard in philosophy,*

2. See Girard 2006, p. 4.

insofar as it is possible to speak of Platonism in very different domains—as when, for instance, Putnam makes it his target of criticism in ethics[3]—and perhaps as something characterizing a general posture of mind. In order to make sense of this generalized Platonism, we should ask what is truly characteristic of the attitude Girard makes fun of in his picturesque description. As he described it, Platonism about the integers comes down to *considering them independently of their (actual) use.* As trophies pinned to our metaphysical wall they are simply *useless.*

Considered thus, they are *no longer* what they really are—they are no longer *numbers.* A number is something with which one can calculate. To consider it independently of the calculations in which it plays a part is not only to *abstract* it, as some philosophers are prone to say, but to entirely *miss* what it is—for, being a number, *that is what it is meant for.* Thus, the very nature of number comes to the fore in the calculations we make using it. A kind of number is defined by a method of calculation, and one might say that there are *as many different kinds of numbers as there are diverse ways of calculating with numbers.* A possible response to the traditional question of whether or not the concept of 'number' is univocal, a question already triggered by the invention of irrational numbers in antiquity, is just to say: *look at what you're doing with them!*

In this sense, the meaning of a number is determined by *its—mathematical—use.* It cannot be discerned apart from it. A number can certainly belong to a mathematical theory, but it belongs to a *mathematical practice* as well, insofar as, at least at some level, one cannot separate mathematical theory and mathematical practice. As a rule, in mathematics a theory defines a set of *possible operations* (or transformations).

This is not to say that numbers do not exist—that they are merely artefacts of use. The inference from the destabilization of the Platonic picture to a revisionary and reductive intuitionist position is in no way obligatory. 'Use' is not something to which anything else

3. See Putnam 2005.

can 'be reduced.' *Where there is use, there is something that is used.* To give pride of place to *the (mathematical) use of numbers* when making sense of what numbers are is not, therefore, to deny that numbers are legitimate citizens of the mathematical world nor even that they are 'objects.' It is to highlight the particular conditions of their objectivity—of their *diverse* objectivity. In contrast, Platonism consists in *rendering these objects useless, that is, bereft of use.*

In saying that Platonism renders the objects whose existence it affirms useless I do not mean to say that it deprives them of any *practical* utility, as if mathematical meaning essentially depended on the possibility of an extra-mathematical application. Perhaps extra-mathematical applications are far more important to mathematics than they are usually taken to be, to the extent that they are very often part of mathematical meaning itself. However, in this case, one might suspect that, ultimately, the alleged 'extra-mathematical' application indeed turns out to be mathematical; and that we should revise our view about what is mathematical—as opposed to 'non-mathematical'—in the initial story we tell.[4]

Nonetheless, if any kind of utility is at issue here, it is *utility in the context of a mathematical practice.* Or more precisely—since 'utility' inappropriately suggests some kind of transcendent end that it helps us to reach—the mere fact of *being used in such a practice.* Platonism literally makes things 'use-less' insofar as it cuts them off from their use, leaving them hanging on the wall of trophies. In other words, Platonism is the ontological counterpart to the attitude that, according to Wittgenstein, philosophers usually adopt toward language: language as it is when it 'goes on holiday.' Analogously or perhaps it is just *the same thing*—Platonism can be viewed as the objectual side of the essentialization of meaning. It invites us to look at objects independently of any definite usages through which we can actually refer to those objects. Or, at the very least, it is the mythology of *a super-usage that goes beyond our ordinary ones.*

4. On this topic, see Benoist 2013.

Of course, this story is not restricted to mathematics. One could even say that it is only incidentally about mathematics; since the whole point is that for it *mathematical practice does not matter.* As such, 'mathematical Platonism' is clearly paradigmatic of a much more general tendency which we can call *'the metaphysical mind.'* Indeed, throughout the history of philosophy this fantasy concerning mathematical ontology has often been used to set the tone of metaphysics more generally. Following the path staked out by our analysis of mathematical Platonism, we can give the following characterization of the metaphysical mind: *it claims to get at how things are 'independently of any way of dealing with them.'* Thus, the prevalence of ontology in a classical sense of the term is characteristic of the metaphysical mind. It holds that every question can and should be turned into an *ontological* one—as though questions of ontology were independent of any more *specific* questions.

Questioning the legitimacy of such a project should be a top priority in the present philosophical situation. The return of metaphysics understood as substantial ontology—something independent of epistemology and semantics, and to some extent prior to them—is a blatant fact of contemporary philosophy. This is true on both sides of the crumbling wall that is still supposed to divide the worlds of 'Analytic' and 'Continental' philosophy. Our time is marked by a craving for ontology that, one way or another, must apparently be quenched. Contrary to many philosophers who, on either side of the divide, are nowadays willing to sate this urge, I personally prefer the therapeutic option.

What is wrong with ontology? In fact, the answer would be 'nothing' if it did what it is supposed to do: *genuinely* address the question of *what there is.* However, this question comes with a cost and, in order to tackle it seriously, one must be aware of the conditions under which it can be correctly formulated. The problem with what is usually called 'ontology' is that it attempts to formulate the question *unconditionally.* Ontology is essentially *de-contextualized ontology,* the quest for an acontextual description of what there is. In contrast, the ordinary question about what there is does not call for an answer to the question about what there is *in general*, but only what there is from a particular point of view and in a particular situation. Therefore, it might not be a (purely) ontological question in the traditional sense of the term.

Now, this is not to say that everything in the current 'ontological turn' should be discarded. There are, of course, good reasons for this development that can be found in the history of Analytic philosophy after the Second World War. The revival of 'metaphysics' understood as 'ontology' in Analytic philosophy at the end of the twentieth century should be assessed against the backdrop of the dominance of the semantic perspective in the immediately preceding era. From this point of view the ontological turn may be a genuine step forward. It is expressive of the striving for a more substantial conception of truth according to which the world is not merely what I am talking about, let alone what I say about it, but has structures of its own which I may capture if I am speaking adequately.

What does 'adequacy' mean here? It means that thought, thus, exerts a genuine grip on the world. It does not stop short of it but gives it to us *as it is*, in its being as it exists independently of thought. This 'realistic' constraint is something that we shall want to retain from the 'ontological turn.' Our language and the thought that it expresses are not cut off from the world they refer to, but instead plough deep normative furrows in that very world, determining what should count as *this* or *that*—which of course requires that first something *be* in order for it to count as being this or that.

On the other hand, what is thus captured is not merely what is spoken of or thought about, but *some being*, one that usually has other properties than simply being spoken of or thought about. Indeed, to speak and think is most commonly to speak and think of those 'other properties.' Thus, overcoming the merely 'semantic' perspective—one which considers things simply as correlates of utterances or thoughts[5]—does not mean that we have to open some

---

5. For the sake of argument, I pretend here that there is no difference, but in fact there is: it is not at all clear that it makes sense to speak of *the 'correlate' of a thought*. More precisely, there is no such thing as *mental semantics*.

kind of 'back door' in order to reach 'the things themselves' that exist beyond language or thought. To some degree it comes down to *taking language and thought seriously*—taking seriously their actual commitment to reality.

Consequently, the issue of 'realism' correctly understood has nothing to do with the preposterous debate between so-called 'correlationism' and 'anti-correlationism' that is characteristic of the last stage of what is called 'Continental thought.' What would happen to the world if I disappeared, as I surely will? It would certainly remain the same, barring a few details. However, though independent of me, it would still be exactly what I imagine it would be: 'the world without me.' Being overwhelmed by the world is a possible *attitude* we can take toward the world. As uncomfortable as that attitude can be, it is certainly, in some sense of 'metaphysics,' a genuinely *metaphysical* but not in any case ontological issue.[6]

The point is this: giving full weight to the reality of what is talked or thought about is not to abstract from talking or thinking. On the contrary, in order to make sense of 'reality' we should focus on how we talk and think about it, on *our actual ways* of doing that.[7] Not that our talk or thought 'determines reality,' as is sometimes said. But it does *make it count in some way.* And reality is exactly *what, in one way or another, counts.* Addressing reality is not merely a matter of listing entities from a perspective gained by peering through the backdoor of the museum of 'useless' objects. It does not consist in the construction of *acontextual lists,* but rather the consideration of the various *uses—actual uses*—through which we genuinely come to grips with reality.

The big mistake of modern relativism is in thinking that, because reality is necessarily described according to a particular standard of

6. To understand the kind of distinction between metaphysics and ontology that I make here, see Benoist 2014.

7. Incidentally this was Plato's own method, as opposed to what goes by the name of 'Platonism' in recent philosophy.

usage, it is for that reason *less real.* This view also embodies a mistake about the nature of 'use,' for it proceeds as if uses of words did not take place in the world, as if they were not so many ways to orientate ourselves in reality, and thus, to be engaged with it.[8] An alternative picture is this: thinking is essentially *something we do.* That does not mean that thinking is simply reduced to background practices that are not themselves instances of *thinking,* but more that thinking is itself a practice, *a conceptual practice*—a real way of proceeding. In the proper sense of the term, there are *ways of thinking.*

To give an example of the sense of 'reality' that thus emerges, we can focus on the case of quantum mechanics.

The blatant problem with quantum mechanics is that it seems to be at odds with our traditional and familiar sense of objectivity. Usually, we take it that objects satisfy definite conditions of individuation. Identity is not a property that some objects happen to have; rather, objects are defined in terms of *the kind of identity* they possess. One might say that, to some degree, objects are simply operators of identification: to be an 'object' is to remain the same in different circumstances.

Now, part of this idea of sameness seems to be a capacity on the part of objects to be kept track of. One has only to ask oneself the following: Would the objects that we single out, point at and name in our ordinary life still qualify as objects if it were never possible to keep track of them? To reiterate, this is not a *property* of objects, but rather part of their definition, a *grammatical feature* of our talk of 'objects.'

The problem is that it seems as though there cannot be any 'objects' in quantum mechanics, for it is impossible to simultaneously know both the position and the speed of a 'particle.' Thus, I cannot 'track' a particle in the ordinary sense of the word that is connected to the traditional notion of an 'object.' The upshot of this is that a lot

8. In a sense of 'engaged' that may not be far from that used by John McDowell in McDowell 2009.

of philosophers endorse an idealistic interpretation of quantum mechanics. Because what QM says about reality does not seem to be compatible with the traditional picture of reality as made up of objects, it is very tempting to think that QM simply does not concern reality. As such, quantum entities, *which are not objects*—do not have the kind of individuation characteristic of objects—they are a sort of construction, an ideal product.

Now, there are seemingly two solutions to this problem.

The first holds that, beyond the ostensible *tensorial* structure of quantum entities, one that *projects* but does not *factorize*, there are 'real objects'—that is, entities which *do* satisfy the conditions of individuation constitutive of objects—that we simply do not have access to. To make them visible, therefore, we either have to *interpret* our formalism, giving ourselves diverse ranges of objects or even diverse worlds—the 'multiple interpretation' strategy—or else *complete* the formalism by introducing objects where on first inspection there were none to be found: this is the 'hidden variables' strategy. Nowadays a good part of the philosophical discussion about QM focuses on one or other of these perspectives, although neither seems to make a real difference from the physical point of view. However, the issue is a metaphysical one, and its extreme difficulty lies in the fact that it seemingly requires us to repudiate our claim to have knowledge of objects, in a field where objectivity as such matters.

The second jettisons 'realism' as the incongruous cult of objects and endorses an anti-realistic understanding of quantum mechanics. It acknowledges that quantum entities are mere *constructions* and that, here, there are no apples to be picked. (Apple picking being quite a good image for the classical idea of object-hood.) On this view, quantum mechanics *reduces to* its formalism.

I take both pictures to be mistaken. Sticking to the classical model of objectivity and trying to find something like traditional 'objects' beyond and behind the quantum formalism amounts to *not taking QM seriously enough*. That is to say: not respecting its own referential enterprise, and acting as though there were no other form of reference than the mere *denotation of objects.* However, to do the converse, reducing QM to its formalism in aid of an 'anti-realistic' interpretation, is to *not take that formalism seriously:* to ignore it as *a way of thinking,* of exerting a discriminating grip on reality.

What is 'reality' in QM? It is exactly that which is captured by the tensorial formalism QM makes use of. There is no need to translate that formalism into something that lacks its bite, its special contact with reality that cannot be replicated through other means. To substitute anything else for this realism would be to lose sight of the *specific dimension of reality* it allows us to capture.

Now, is it the case—as my friend Thierry Paul argued in a conversation we had about this—that against both classical objectivism and anti-realistic anti-objectivism, I would like to 'place reality in the Hilbert space' (of which QM makes use)? As if it made any sense to say: 'I have *discovered* that Reality (with a big R) is in the Hilbert space'? Of course not. It is very difficult to see what it would mean for reality *in general* to be in a Hilbert space. However, the reality that the quantum physicist is talking about certainly is!

The whole point is that reality is something which we can speak of—or which we can operate on—*in definite ways.* Quantum mechanics is one such way and therefore captures something of reality. It even constitutes a very powerful insight into reality. There are things that cannot be said, or more precisely cannot be made visible, in reality, without using the quantum formalism. 'Made visible' is better because it is not clear that *calculation* as such—and quantum mechanics is essentially calculation—*says* anything. None of this diminishes the fact that calculation *expresses* reality and allows us to see it from a particular point of view, specifically in terms of its dynamics: its capacity to combine and to recombine.

As such, the ordinary tendency to think of 'formalism' always in terms of '*mere* formalism' is incorrect. It is not as though on one side of a divide there lay a (real) object, and on the other something (merely) formal. In highly formalized theories, it is very commonly

the case that formalism is not what people call a 'simple (interme-
diate) calculation,' but is in fact what establishes the cognitive grip
we exercise on reality. To calculate is to think, to forge new paths
into reality.

Now, the point is not that in this context there are no objects, but
some bizarre entities that it is impossible to keep track of. It is more
that *there are genuinely diverse standards of objectivity* that essentially depend on what you are doing with the things you claim exist.
*How one operates with entities is not incidental to the business of
ontology.* The example of quantum mechanics, with the ontological
import of the tensor product, shows that it is simply part of it. However, what is true of QM is also true of 'traditional' ontology: What
sets the standard for traditional 'objects' except *a certain way of operating with identity?*

Thus, the question whether Reality in general is primarily made
up of objects or of any other kind of entity is sheer nonsense if *considered as a general question* (i.e., what people often call an 'ontological
question'). 'Objects' or 'operators' (as found in QM) are different ways
of exerting a cognitive grip on reality, and as such they define different takes on it. Now, each perspective reaches reality itself. Neither
is optional—it is not as if reality itself remained beyond our contem-
plation and so to speak untouched by it—they are *different ways our
knowledge of reality concretely proceeds.* Through their different
paths we can make sense of as many *dimensions* of reality. The
meaning of 'reality' is not impervious to our calculations.

One is of course free to break off the calculation at any time, attempting instead to consider the entities as they allegedly are 'by
themselves.' Such *isolation* is a prerequisite for considering objects
'in themselves' according to a notion of objecthood that belongs to
metaphysics understood as ontology. This is a deeply traditional
philosophical strategy. But what should we think of the 'useless' entities it offers up to us? By abstracting from their use we deprive
them of their meaning, and end up positing beings without being
clear *what* they are.

Placing reality beyond use and *at the same time* trying to make sense of it as what our thinking and knowing concerns—these are the two conflicting claims of traditional metaphysical 'realism'—is to fall prey to a delusion Frege derides: that there is a way to 'wash the fur without getting it wet' *(den Pelz waschen, ohne ihn nass zu machen)*.[9] If you want to make sense of 'reality,' keep it real! Get your fur soaking wet! Do not be afraid of calculations.

9. Frege 1974, §26. Of course, it is significant that this German idiom is used in order to designate an *unrealistic claim*, like 'have your cake and eat it' in English.

CHAPTER ELEVEN

Unshadowed Realism

NEW REALISM is certainly a *fact.* At the beginning of the twenty-first century diverse philosophers in different countries call themselves 'realists' in a converging manner.[1] However, the very label provokes certain worries. Every self-proclaimed novelty sounds somewhat suspicious from the point of view of philosophy. Fashion is not an intellectual criterion. If this realism is so 'new,' doesn't it run the risk of merely amounting to a series of superficial paradoxes that are at odds with reality—surely the worst outcome for any 'realism'? It would be presumptuous to think that reality has remained concealed despite the efforts of so many generations of researchers, so that only we, at last, have managed to uncover it. All in all, it seems quite unlikely that any realism could be considered 'new.'

Indeed, perhaps realism *must not* be new—for novelty might turn out to be incompatible with the basic characteristic of realism: *being true to reality.* Reality, as such, remains what it is. This is a *definition* of reality. Isn't it therefore suspicious that a philosophical discourse that claims to be the discourse of 'reality' also claims to be new? Isn't it logical that this discourse aims at capturing philosophically *that which has always been?* So a tension may arise between the ambition of telling a—radically—new story and the claim that the object of this story is *eternal.* Why should there be anything new to say about reality? Doesn't this contradict the concept of reality itself?

1. See Ferraris 2014 and Gabriel 2014.

One natural response to this objection is to point out that *reality has changed*. Perhaps, at this moment in time, reality raises new problems. Perhaps 'New Realism' is characterized by the fact that it addresses these issues—in contrast to 'Old Realism' that of course *didn't have to deal with them*. Perhaps for that very reason we shall find that 'Old Realism' *isn't able* to deal with them when its framework is applied to our novel context.

Indeed, it is fashionable to adopt this attitude. In the age of the internet it is a widespread conviction that our reality become essentially 'virtual,' exactly as it is supposed to have become *immaterial*—at least in developed countries—during the age of deindustrialization. However, upon closer examination this picture is extremely suspect. Cyber-democracy will be possible only if there is democracy outside the net, and it will only be a means to or aspect of this 'real' democracy. Moreover, the computer of the postmodern intellectual, so dear to this 'new form of democracy,' will always have to be built by someone—if only by a robot. Of course, we live, as we always have, in a real, material world. The bullshit typed out by the postmodern intellectual on his or her computer about the derealization of this world in no way diminishes this fact.

Is it so obvious, in the end, that 'reality has changed,' as the apologists of postmodernity like to say? Even to the point that it is not 'reality' anymore? No. Reality remains—and will always remain—reality. Of course, there are new things and non-things in it, some of which it may prove difficult to think of as *realities*—a situation which may put our concept of reality under some strain, compelling us to revise it *locally*. This is probably one aspect of what so-called New Realism is concerned with. However, this does not alter the global concept of reality. Why would we call it 'reality' otherwise? And how could New *Realism* deserve its name if it was not about reality in the same sense in which realism has always claimed to be? However, if the generic sense of reality that has always been at stake for realism is also at stake for it, then it just is *realism*—even if it concerns newer, potentially paradoxical, forms of reality.

Now even if realism can, in *essence,* be no newer than its object, it remains the case that a particular form of realism might turn out to be *historically* new. On this understanding New Realism would be new insofar as, as an intellectual stance, it breaks with the dominant view of the previous intellectual generation. Isn't it in fact striking that a series of thinkers more or less educated in the context of so-called 'Continental Philosophy' in the broad sense, has recently come to call themselves realists? We can say at the very least that this label used to be highly unpopular in this tradition, diverse though it may have been. Even today, one finds huge resistance to it in this part of the philosophical world.

As a whole, what is usually called—by its adversaries—Continental Philosophy (CP) developed on the basis of very strong anti-realist assumptions and has thus far been characterized by a strongly anti-realist philosophical stance. Things may have turned out differently, for in the tradition from which CP takes its inspiration there have been strongly realist metaphysicians, Baruch de Spinoza being one of them. Nevertheless, in its way of reading classical works—reading being an important part of what philosophy consists in according to the conception of philosophy CP advocates—CP is essentially *anti-realist.*

As such, the adoption of the realist theme certainly constitutes a sea change in CP's history. However, New Realism should not be reduced to a palace revolution in the internal history of CP. In the first place, a characteristic feature of the exponents of New Realism is that, although usually educated in the Continental tradition, they are more or less acquainted with the argumentative style, as well as certain parts of the content of, Analytic Philosophy (AP). In different ways and to various degrees they stand at the crossroads between the philosophical traditions. At the very least they demonstrate that there is some kind of contamination of one tradition by the other: an alteration, as it were, of the Continental tradition by means of the Analytic style of philosophy. This is certainly one aspect of the historic 'novelty' of New Realism.

Secondly, New Realism claims to break with far more than the anti-realism—maybe we can call it the *idealism*—characteristic of the Continental tradition: it claims to aspire to a *global* break with the intellectual mood of the previous philosophical generation. For it is clear that, as popular as the theme of 'realism' might have been in the Analytic tradition, it would be entirely wrong to characterize AP *as a whole* as adopting a realist stance. If the origins of AP have a strongly realist flavour—whether in Frege or the British philosophy of the early twentieth century which broke with British Idealism—nevertheless, by the time it reached its postwar 'classical age' it had entered a strongly anti-realist era. This anti-realism was characteristic of its semantic phase, when, even as it purported to be realist, it essentially placed the world at a *distance from us*, something which we could access only by *referring* to it—as though there were always a referential distance between us and the world. In fact, AP had its own struggle to recover the thought that things, even when we speak of them and even *in* speaking of them, are not mere objects of reference but things that possess *other ways of being* (than to be referred to) just as we have more ways of relating to them than merely referring to them.

So it seems that by the end of the twentieth century contemporary philosophy *as a whole* had wound up in the position of having to once more secure its grip on the world. To some extent New Realism can be considered a response to this epochal situation.

What must the core of New Realism be if it is to earn its realist title? The basic tenet of every realism is clearly expressed by Aristotle in his famous affirmation:

> It is not because we think that you are white, that you *are* white, but because you are white we who say this have the truth.[2]

This saying expounds not only the *independence* of reality (*Socrates's being white*, for example) relative to truth and knowledge, but also the *priority* of the former in relation to the latter. *First* Socrates is

2. Aristotle, *Metaphysics*, Θ, 1051b 6–9, in Aristotle 1984, vol. 2, p. 1660.

white. *Only then*, does it make sense for us to think that he is white—and for what we think, when we think this, to be true. The Philosopher even describes the relation between them as one of *grounding*: it is *because of* Socrates's being white that what we think is true when we think that he is white.

Thus we get, it seems, the basic idea of a full-blooded—as opposed to *illusory*—realism, that is, the ontological grounding of truth. What is true or not depends fundamentally on *how things are*. Let us call it *reality*. Without this point there is no realism.

Difficulties clearly arise at this juncture. A postmodern intellectual will ask why, in Aristotle's example, it particularly matters that I am 'white'—and what, after all, is a 'white man'? In so doing, *she will absolutely be right*. The categories we are using and the simple fact that we are using them raise many issues, especially in this sort of example. Just ask the main character of *Light in August*. As such the critical analyses of the twentieth century are genuinely valuable, and so I warn my New Realist friends against restoring immutable 'ontological' categories—with all their semantic blindness—too hastily. In other words, do not throw out the baby of *criticism* with the bathwater of postmodern relativism!

The point of realism, however, is not that various aspects of reality are simple to identify or that our identifications of them cannot be controversial or raise various issues. It is that *when we succeed* in constructing a working identification of some part of reality in a given context, what we capture in so doing exists independently of our identifying it and is exactly what it is, whether we identify it or not. Reality is what it is. As we said above, this is its *definition*.

This is the wisdom of 'Old' Realism. New Realism will want, unless it has stolen its name, to preserve this immutable truth against—I hope—every manner of modern, postmodern, or postpostmodern insanity.

The question then is, what could be 'new' about 'realism'? It seems to me that the two leading figures of the movement known as New

Realism proffer two different possible views of what constitutes the genuine 'novelty' of New Realism, in contrast to the ancient or the, let us say, *classical* one.

One of these leading figures, Markus Gabriel, appears to hold that the characteristic feature of the new realism is that it embraces what I would call an *ultra-intentional ontology.* According to Gabriel, *everything exists except the world.*[3] This staunch denial of the existence of the world is certainly meant to sound paradoxical and, at first sight, seems to conflict with any kind of realist commitment. On closer reflection, however, the ostensible paradox vanishes, as we find here some kind of Kantian argument: whether or not I say that something exists, it can do so only in the world; therefore what sense does it make to say that 'the world exists'?

One can then observe that saying the world *does not exist* makes no more sense than saying it does. Or, at the very least, it is a *categorial negation.* It states that the world is not the kind of thing of which it makes sense to say that it exists—perhaps because it is not, fundamentally, a 'thing' at all. In fact, nihilism about the world—the affirmation that 'the world is *nothing'*—could boil down to this *grammatical point.* There is no need, however, to quibble over words. It is, after all, a question of philosophical style.

That said, behind Gabriel's affirmation that 'the world does not exist,' there is likely something more substantial: that is, a principled *critical stance against metaphysics,* the idea that it makes no sense to talk of existence *in general* or *globally.* This point can be generalized: *'reality'* does not exist or make sense absolutely, only *real things* do. The grammar of reality is precisely that of 'real things.' As such, investigating reality consists in taking a look at real things in all their particularity (which does not exclude looking at their generality)—not in espousing an overall view of reality.

This point is extremely important. Indeed it is *critical,* for I am not convinced that all the New Realists share Gabriel's conception.

3. Gabriel 2015a.

In fact, it appears that *the craving for metaphysics* plays a very important role in the present revival of realism. Philosophers want once again to provide us with grand pictures of the world. These pictures go beyond what even the previous generation, and perhaps that of recent centuries, had thought to be within the conditions of possibility—not to mention the lines of 'no trespass'—that constrain such accounts. We can distinguish two schools of thought relating to this issue within the New Realist camp: on the one hand there are those for whom realism is just a name for metaphysics and the promised return of 'realism' means the unleashing of speculative metaphysical ambitions of any kind; on the other hand there are those who do not want to develop a fully-fledged metaphysical system in the name of realism—and who perhaps even consider this task impossible or nonsensical—but who simply want to do justice to the diverse kinds of *real things* that we, as human beings, have dealings with.

If I understand Markus Gabriel's work correctly, he stands much more in the latter camp—even if, sometimes, he adopts the language of the other 'realist' camp, possibly in order to let himself be understood by them. I am very sympathetic to this, as I personally think that metaphysics in the speculative sense is not only *not required* by realism but that it is the main *obstacle* to a genuine realism—to a philosophical stance that makes sense of 'real things.' Thus, what I feel uncomfortable with in Gabriel's statement is not the idea that the world does not exist—once this bold assertion is adequately interpreted—but the idea that *everything else does exist.*

A traditional problem concerning the nature of realism surfaces at this point. One might think that realism consists merely in saying that *certain things exist*, and in such a way that the more things you say exist, the more of a realist you are. By this standard—at least if we allow ourselves to tamper with existence and to make room for some kind of 'there-being' *(es gibt)* on our (meta-)ontological shelves—Alexius von Meinong should be thought of as the most realist philosopher of them all. Now, as a matter of fact, he was a genuinely realist philosopher, but his realism seems to have been misguided. Realism cannot consist in allowing that things that do not exist in fact do—even in some watered-down sense of 'existence.'[4] In fact, a capacity *to distinguish between what does and does not exist in context* seems to be a basic requirement of genuine realism.

So when Markus Gabriel appears to affirm that the distinctive feature of 'New Realism'—as opposed to the 'ancient' kind—is that according to it *'everything exists,'* this raises a genuine issue. If this assertion primarily means, as it seems to, that New Realism countenances every kind of 'intentional object' as a part of reality, it could turn out to be very difficult to swallow *qua* realism. Should we say that the unicorn exists? Gabriel's answer to this question is that *in mythology it does*. However, the 'fields of sense'[5] theory looks very similar to the traditional *semantic* position—is the unicorn's existence anything more than mere 'existence-in-the-discourse'? Now, the mere fact that the unicorn exists 'in my discourse' does not make it *exist*—this blunt contrast between a merely semantic existence and real existence is another version of what I have described as the basic tenet of realism. By extending the concept of existence so far, Gabriel seems to render it incredibly fragile.

However, there remains a difference. Gabriel's 'fields of sense' are full-blooded *ontological fields*. They not only commit us to an existence 'in the discourse' but also to the existence of *a genuine aspect of things*. Hence the example of *seeing Vesuvius:* the particular aspect Vesuvius has when viewed from a particular perspective is not merely a subjective product of my vision, but an objective dimension of the reality of Vesuvius itself.

This example raises a whole host of issues, for it treats perception as though it *meant* something; indeed, as though it were a good

---

4. Of course a Meinongian could reply that Meinong precisely does not say that what does not exist *exists*. However, he still treats what does not exist as an *entity*, and that is the problem.

5. See Gabriel 2015b.

example of how so much of what is meant is actually part of the thing itself. We should obviously discuss whether perception really means anything[6]—in fact, making sense of the 'reality' of the perceived is an essential step in the necessary clarification of what realism is. But at any rate, this example gives a good idea of Gabriel's realism: the realism of *an ontologically loaded semantics—or a semantically loaded ontology, as you prefer.*

This realism is explicitly introduced by its author as an amendment to Frege, whom he holds responsible for a good part of the entrenched idealism in AP. By objectifying the Kantian universe of representations and making them 'senses' *(Sinne)* Frege still maintains the idea of an intermediary between us and the world. On the contrary, according to the picture that Gabriel advocates, our meaning commits us to the world 'directly,' for it has an immediate ontological import. In its variety, it discloses to us as many dimensions as the world itself contains. This analysis of the essentially *ontological* orientation of meaning is surely realist in its basis. I certainly do not want to question the idea—one to which I am very sympathetic—of a tight connection between meaning and reality. However, *as it is stated,* this good idea might nonetheless have some undesirable consequences.

The problem is that the formulation of this position invites an extreme ontological liberalism that, paradoxically, sounds postmodern in spite of its realist commitments. If everything exists, then *nothing exists*—that is, nothing can seriously be said to exist. When Gabriel says that Little Red Riding Hood at least exists in her fairy tale, it is difficult not to think that he is confusing real being with intentional being—in fact, he seems to be *willingly* confusing them. However, *although the story of Little Red Riding Hood exists, Little Red Riding Hood does not.*

Of course, one might be motivated to ascribe some kind of 'reality' to intentional objects by the fact that fiction is not entirely cut

6. See Travis 2004.

off from reality but can in fact only be understood in relation to it; something that is true, in one way or another, of every mental attitude. Realism cannot stop short of embracing fiction or, for that matter, any kind of mental attitude or accomplishment. However, to think that ascribing a *reality* to intentional entities is a good way of dealing with fiction's real engagement with reality is simply mistaken. It overlooks *the essentially normative character* of intentional attitudes that constitutively orients them toward reality; reality itself, that is—not 'intentional reality.'[7]

If I expect someone, it is *the (real) fact* that she arrives that fulfils my expectation, just as it is *the (real) fact* that she does not arrive that disappoints the same expectation. My expectation sets, as it were, a standard for reality to which it either does or does not conform. This is true of every intentional attitude. Now, it might be tempting to treat this standard as an *object in its own right*. In which case my expected friend—like the 'imaginary friend' of children—might be thought to exist, or 'subsist,' or something else I know not what, independently of the real friend I actually have. Or, in an apparently—but only apparently—more subtle way, independently of my sheer lack of friends. This is, however, to forget the *normativity* of the intentional attitude's content. What is my 'expected friend,' if not *a measure I can apply to reality*, so that if someone comes along, it makes sense to see whether or not she is the friend I'm expecting? What is a so-called 'intentional object' except a *device for identifying things?*

Of course, there are a wide variety of devices possessing multifarious uses. A child's 'imaginary friend' does not claim to be real in the same way as my expected friend and perhaps does not claim to be real at all. However, even in the latter case, the imaginary friend is not another kind of friend—an *unreal* friend—but something that makes sense only insofar as it expresses an aspect of the child's relation to reality. You do not see reality in the same way when you have

7. See Benoist 2008.

'imaginary friends.' For all that imaginary friends are not a part of reality, but are instead *our relation to reality, inasmuch as in this relation reality itself—and nothing else—is at stake.* The final proviso adds the realist touch here. We do not need *intentional entities* in order to be realists. Quite the opposite: such entities would cut us off from reality. We need *intentionality to be constitutively involved with reality,* which is something else entirely.

Thus, if the novelty of 'New Realism' consists in an extreme liberalism that countenances all manner of entities whether they are traditionally held to be real or not, perhaps we should just stick to Old Realism—which had a 'robust sense of reality.'

However, a different interpretation of New Realism's alleged novelty is suggested by Maurizio Ferraris.[8] One part of Ferraris's crusade in favour of New Realism is his strong criticism of the typical postmodern challenge to the autonomy of the physical world. Postmodernism is essentially a *culturalism.* It tends to deny that the physical world—what we call 'nature'—has any reality of its own. Everything is culturally determined from the outset, and thus falls prey to relativism.

According to Ferraris, we should, *contra* this relativism, account for the robustness of *first nature,* a robustness in which—and this is a noteworthy aspect of Ferraris's thought—*perception* as such participates. Against the common theme of theory-ladenness, Ferraris has indeed endorsed a very robust perceptual realism drawing upon the resources provided by the Italian school of Gestalt psychology.[9] This is all well and good: questioning the autonomy of nature has indeed been an important aspect of postmodern anti-realism and excessive anti-naturalism should certainly be blocked if we want to make sense of reality as such. *For nature is part of reality as well.*

8. See Ferraris 2014.
9. This aspect comes to the fore in Ferraris's formulation of his turn to realism in Ferraris 2001.

'As well'—not *only*. Here is where the difficulties begin. Ferraris identifies the novelty of New Realism as consisting in its making room for *social reality as something 'constructed.'* Thus, we stumble upon intentionality once again, although likely for different reasons this time. Ferraris is probably right in saying that traditional realism had missed the fact that social reality is constructed. I will return to this point at the end. It is characteristic of 'Old Realism' to treat social reality as a kind of *'nature,'* as if it were somehow independent of what human beings do. This is what Postmoderns have criticized, quite rightly, under the label of 'essentialism.' Not everything is 'nature' in this limited sense of the term.

Now, the problem might lie in the word 'construction.' What does it mean? If one says, with Ferraris and many other contemporary ontologists,[10] that social reality is 'constructed,' doesn't one run the risk of drawing too sharp a contrast between natural and social reality from the point of view of their shared 'reality'? Let us be clear: these kinds of reality certainly differ. However, are they different considered *as parts of reality?* In saying that one of them is 'constructed,' we run the risk of making it appear 'less real' than the other. It is as if there were firstly the 'real reality'—nature—and then built on top of it an artificial construct, only possessing *the reality we ourselves gave it.* In other words: *as if modern idealism is, at least at some level, correct.*

Now, I think—and I suppose Ferraris should be inclined to think it as well—that *modern idealism is wrong at every level.* Social reality is not *less* real than natural reality. At most, it is *differently real.* However, in saying this, we should nevertheless not mistake a *difference of genus* for a *difference of category.* Nature and culture are two genera of reality, but they belong to precisely one and the same category: reality.

Is the German state any less real than the German people? And the *German people* less real than the human beings the German

10. Searle being one of them, of course.

people happen to be made up of? It is the German state that declares the war, not the German people. On the other hand if the German state declares war, the young males among them will have no choice but to either go to war or to go to jail, all *because they are Germans*, not because they are human beings. Only something real can have these *consequences*, or be prone to such *effects*. Would it help if a German citizen, in such a situation, tried to argue that he is 'not really' (perhaps only 'intentionally'?) German? Social reality possesses a terrible robustness of its own.

Of course, to some extent, the thought that social reality is constructed can be a way of securing *a kind of reality for it*. If we strip social reality of its constitutive network of conventions and practices there will be little of it left. Denying that it is constructed therefore renders it very fragile. Still, it is unclear that 'construction' is the best word to use here. In fact, it sounds like a concession to the enemy—as if, regarding social reality, *constructivism* were right. Now, constructivism is wrong in this respect, and—since social reality is, so to speak, its natural territory—it is very important to understand why.

No doubt nature is real. But it is not the case that what is beyond nature—the social world—is not real, or less real than nature. The social world is *immediately* real and as real as nature in the sense that it is not up to me to decide whether what is knocking at my door is a policeman or not. And, what is more interesting, neither is it up to '*us*'—the community—to decide. The image of 'decision' is misleading here. Social reality is not the product of a spontaneous collective decision. It is determined rather by the *conventions and shared practices* that structure it, and that let what is part of it *count as what it counts for*. Now, it is not the case that social reality is, metaphysically speaking, a 'naked' reality that requires an extrinsic social determination to be layered onto it, like the icing on the surface of a cake. It is *intrinsically* social, and therefore can only be captured as what it is by precisely this kind of determination. In this case, conventions and shared practices are a crucial part of the *format* of reality itself. The reality of social reality is not to be sought below the level at which 'social' determinations apply.

Of course, this comes at a cost: *the conditions required by these conventions and by the normative framework of these practices must be met.* Does this mean that these determinations are extrinsic to the objects they qualify? Not at all. The characteristic ontological feature of social objects is that certain norms essentially apply to them. These norms can be disputed, and perhaps they are, but that is another question. Social objects anyway *belong to a normative space*—constituted by a great variety of norms that correspond to as many forms of human conduct and judgment.

This, as such, has nothing to do with 'subjective'—even collectively subjective—intentionality. It is not because we all believe that something is legal that it is *really* legal. It has more to do with the institutions of a given society. Without institutions, intentionality is powerless to define the format of social reality. We do not 'project' something social onto a reality that is not 'by itself' already social. We simply engage immediately with that reality as something 'social.'

Now, why should the story concerning *construction* be a tempting one? Probably because of the entrenched idea that the fundamental sense of 'reality' is that of 'physical reality.' However, this belief is absurd: the majority of the real things that play a part in our lives are not physical things—or at least not things that are *only* physical.

However, the story about construction might stem from a more serious motivation. Doesn't the point we have just made, that it is essential to social objects that some particular norms apply to them, seem to undermine their full-blooded reality? Reality *simpliciter* is just *what norms apply to*. As such, it is what it is, whether a norm is applied to it or not. This is what reality is, and it is precisely the fact that reality is impervious to norms that makes them logically possible as such: the norms are meaningful only insofar as they are capable of applying to reality as it is independently of themselves—as 'being what it is,' whatever the norms might happen to be. Such complete independence does not seem to make sense in the case of social objects.

Of course, whether or not it is correct to describe someone's behaviour as 'fair' depends in no way on the fact that I or anyone else—perhaps even *everyone* else—describe it as such. If it did then it would make no sense to attempt to apply the concept 'fair,' considered as a norm. However, neither would it make sense to apply this norm if the object were not already *treated* in a certain way. For example, if I reduce *this behaviour* to a physical movement, I cannot assess whether or not it is 'fair.' Therefore, it can seem *as if something must already be judged* in order to be that which features in other judgments. On this account, it seems, social realism is not realism 'pure and simple'—'realism of the objects as they are'—but realism of objects as they have already been judged. Let us call this: *'intentional realism.'*

However, this analysis is crippled by a grammatical mistake. It is as if we had to *first* construct the social object through a judgment or a practice before being able to apply any given norm to it—this norm only being applicable to something that has already been rendered suitable for such application. But this is not the way it works. The fact that the object is measured according to a social standard is not something settled before *the judgments we make about it on particular occasions,* or before *we concretely deal with it in a definite context.* It is through such judgments and deeds that the object is determined as being social, as well as the kind of social object it is. There are no meta-judgments or 'constitutive' a priori judgments. Rather, the object possesses a reality that is measured in context by the ordinary judgments we make of it. Now, the fact that a particular object is 'social' is certainly not a mere detail, just one among the many things that we take to be true of it. It is more a *grammatical feature,* one expressed by the way in which we take many things to be true of this object and many others to be false: in the way we talk, think, and deal with it. It has been suggested that we can define the social world in terms of its normativity, but this normativity consists in nothing else than the fact that we are concretely justified in applying certain kinds of norms (teleological, axiological, etc.) to objects of the social world when forming judgments concerning them in a given context. Thus, the 'intrinsic' normativity of these objects is found only in their reality: it is made manifest only when we actually capture and determine that very reality in applying the norms to it that we do.

This reality, like all reality, just is what it is and the norms we apply to it capture it as being just that—not merely as something 'normed by these norms.' However (and this is the point about it being 'essentially' normed) it is by applying norms to social reality *in a very systematic way*—grammar as the measure of *what we actually do* with norms comes into play here—that we capture *what it is*.

Thus, what is 'social' is *genuinely* social and *real as social*. It is not first real in some other way before becoming social, nor need it necessarily be real in any *other* way at all. In the case of many objects and aspects of social reality—one must go further than the category of 'object' in order to make full sense of reality—there is no particular part of the physical world with which it would be meaningful to identify them. The 'social' norms applied to them capture their reality directly. Of course, this means that these aspects of reality are still what they are independently of the fact that we are currently applying norms to them—this is the central point concerning their 'reality.' However, that means we cannot capture their full reality without applying the normative framework *as a whole*. If I treat a corpse as a mere physical body then its social *reality*—its being something that should be buried, etc.—is simply invisible. One who does this has closed one's mind to a whole *dimension* of reality. For reality, as such, has *dimensions*. This is the lesson of 'grammar' that there are many diverse ways of speaking and judging. Every univocal understanding of reality is *grammatically blind*: we have different ways of speaking of reality and judging it to be, and that diversity is essential to the very concept of reality.

If the notion of 'construction' is simply meant to indicate that the concept of 'social reality' presupposes that there exists a *human society*—or at least some kind of society—then it is unobjectionable. That is the crux of the idea of 'social reality.' If it is supposed to suggest that social reality is any less real or is differently real than an allegedly more basic, physical reality, then it is objectionable. 'Reality' is not a concept that defines one kind of thing in contrast to another, or that applies to different kinds of things to differing degrees. It is a *categorial* concept that guarantees that something is what it is independently of whether I am able to find the adequate norm to capture it. From this perspective, social realities are those that can be captured only in social terms. Of course, this means that social reality presupposes society—which is not exactly surprising. Only a metaphysician who feels free to bracket society—placing himself, as it were, outside of the social world and *so outside of reality*—could turn this fact into a problem.

The real issue—and the possible bone of contention between *metaphysical* and *non-metaphysical versions of New Realism*—is whether reality should be considered 'from without' or 'from within.' Or, more precisely, whether it even makes sense to consider it 'from without.' The recurrent worry about 'social reality' may turn out to be merely a symptom of this general problem. It is the characteristic ailment of a philosophy that thinks it makes sense to step back from reality and think, as it were, with one foot in it and the other foot out.

Now, if the novelty of New Realism consists in thinking of social reality as 'constructed' then, once again, a relevant question is whether we should not stick to the 'old' realism, *at least, that is, if it can be described as follows:*

Reality just is what it is—this is its definition. That is what *reality* is, whatever kind of 'reality' it might be. As such, it can never be 'constructed.' However, there are, of course, diverse kinds of reality. And, for some of them, belonging to a *normative* framework—for example, being endowed with *value*—turns out to be essential. Nevertheless, this is something that is manifest in the very ways we apply these norms to parts of reality, for in applying them we treat those parts of reality as essentially being such as to have these norms applied to them. In other words: what can be captured in *this* normative framework cannot be captured any other way. In changing our point of view we simply change our grip on reality; we shift from one to another of its *dimensions*—one in which it makes no sense to attempt recovery of that 'same' part of reality.

Now, in concluding, we can inquire whether the 'Old' Realism was ever really like this. Perhaps the fact that it wasn't—or wasn't entirely—might finally explain the point of pursuing a 'New' Realism.

Let us try to contrast Old Realism with a potentially new version in a slightly different way. There is certainly a substantial kernel of truth in Ferraris's idea that the novelty of New Realism consists in the fact that it considers social reality to be 'constructed.' The idea perhaps becomes clearer if we reformulate it: New Realism targets the view according to which *the norms that are characteristic of social being are not constructed.* Now, the view thus targeted might indeed be one aspect of 'Old Realism.' For that realism seemed to want—at least in its most conservative forms—to make the norms characterizing social reality *a merely real part of social reality*, as if norms were somehow imprinted onto reality independently of the fact that we make judgments about it and more generally have dealings with it.

However, this is probably one aspect of a more global problem. According to 'Old Realism'—and this is possibly what makes it 'old'—norms as such are *part of reality itself.* This means that when we succeed in applying a norm to something, it is because this norm is already to be found in the structure of the thing itself. Reality, as such, has a normative character. Old realism, from this point of view, is an anthropomorphic realism. (Which does not prevent it from also being a theocentric realism—but that might itself prove to be a form of disguised anthropomorphism.) In fact, one aspect of this anthropomorphism is *intentionalism*. Old Realism was apt to think that reality itself did our job for us, that it already contained within itself the norms we try to apply to it.

Now, *norms are precisely our responsibility*. Perhaps this might be the whole point of a genuine 'New Realism': making clear and keeping in view the categorial gulf between norms and reality. A part of reality can bear a norm in virtue of the fact that we *use* it for that purpose. A part of reality can also be such that *it is essential that a particular norm applies to it*. However, even in these cases—both of which are important in order to make full sense of reality—*it is never the case that norm and reality are one and the same thing*. They remain categorially different. Reality just is what it is. As such, it can conform to a given norm (or not). On the other hand, a norm, as such, is not a being: it is what adequately or inadequately captures a given class of beings.

Of course, sometimes it makes sense to speak of 'normative beings'—for example in the case of those beings for which it is essential that a certain kind of norm is applicable. If we pretend to capture those beings without making use of these norms, or by simultaneously using other *incompatible* norms, we simply lose track of our object: we can no longer claim to have 'the same reality' in view (or, as a matter of fact, to have *any* reality in view). However, reality and the norm that we apply to it are nevertheless logically distinct.

An easy way to make sense of this point is to focus on the particular norm of 'truth.' Truth and reality are *not the same thing*, even if truth (perhaps not always, e.g., in the case of mathematical or other 'ideal' truths) concerns reality, and often depends on the fact that what is real is in fact real. Of course, there might be *real truth-bearers*—for example *an uttered statement*—but the truths they bear are not real. They merely *characterize what is real*, even if, as is usually the case one way or another, they concern reality. Thus, what matters to the realist, is not that the norm be a *real* part of reality—which, categorially speaking, it cannot be, but that it *really applies to reality*—in other words that reality really conforms to it. That is all that realism amounts to.

Now, the myth according to which norms are *as such* part of reality is not only *not required* by realism—it is a major epistemological *obstacle* to an authentic realism. Treating norms as genuine parts of reality makes reality *less real*, as it were—for it introduces into reality the logical gap that always exists between a norm and what satisfies it. Further, it makes the norm *less normative*—that is to say less capable of measuring a reality from which it no longer possesses the requisite *logical distance*.

This mistake is clearly made with the best of intentions. In projecting norms into reality itself one may take oneself to be securing their capacity to capture and determine reality. However, this move is not only unnecessary but is actually detrimental to realism's aims. By rendering autonomous that which *constitutively cannot be autonomous*, one risks jeopardizing the autonomy of *what is absolutely autonomous*. Overcoming this confusion by making full sense of *reality's independence*—understood in terms of the *category difference between norms and reality*—is the true agenda of a renewed realism. This realism is free of all the shadows that Old Realism thought it necessary to cast over reality; as a consequence it is able to countenance the *diverse dimensions of reality* that are captured by various norms in different contexts.

References

Antonelli, Mauro. 2001. *Seiendes, Bewußtsein, Intentionalität im Frühwerk von Franz Brentano*. Freiburg-München: Alber.

Aristotle. 1984. *The Complete Works of Aristotle: The Revised Oxford Translation*. Edited by Jonathan Barnes. Princeton: Princeton University Press.

Aubenque, Pierre. 1991. "Une occasion manquée: la genèse avortée de la distinction entre 'l'étant' et le 'quelque chose.'" In *Etudes sur le Sophiste de Platon*, edited by Pierre Aubenque, pp. 365–385. Naples: Bibliopolis.

Austin, John L. 1961. *Philosophical Papers*. Oxford: Oxford University Press.

———. 1964. *Sense and Sensibilia*. Reconstructed from manuscript notes by G. J. Warnock. Oxford: Oxford University Press.

Bacon, John. 2011. "Tropes." *The Stanford Encyclopedia of Philosophy (Winter 2011 Edition)*, edited by Edward N. Zalta. http://plato.stanford.edu/archives/win2011/entries/tropes/.

Benoist, Jocelyn. 2008. "Fulfilment." In *Phenomenology as Grammar*, edited by Jesús Padilla Gálvez, pp. 77–96. Frankfurt am Main: Ontos Verlag.

———. 2013. "Appliquer." In *Le formalisme en action. Aspects mathématiques et philosophiques*, edited by Jocelyn Benoist and Thierry Paul, pp. 87–110. Paris: Hermann.

———. 2014. "Apologie de la métaphysique." In *Etudes sur Totalité et Infini*, edited by Danielle Cohen-Levinas and Alexander Schnell, pp. 45–59. Paris: Vrin.

Brandom, Robert. 1994. *Making It Explicit*. Cambridge, MA: Harvard University Press.

Brentano, Franz. 1930. *Wahrheit und Evidenz*, edited by Oskar Kraus. Hamburg: Felix Meiner.

———. 1966. *The True and the Evident*. Translated by Roderick M. Chisholm, Ilse Politzer, and Kurt R. Fischer. London: Routledge.

———. 1973. *Psychology from an Empirical Standpoint*. Translated by Antos C. Rancurello, D. B. Terrell, and Linda McAlister. London: Routledge.

Chrudzimski, Arkadiusz. 2001. *Intentionalitätstheorie beim frühen Brentano*. Dordrecht: Kluwer Academic Publishers.

Courtine, Jean-François. 1990. *Suarez et le système de la métaphysique*. Paris: P.U.F.

———. 2007. *La cause de la phénoménologie*. Paris: P.U.F.

Dutant, Julien, and Pascal Engel. 2005. *Philosophie de la connaissance*. Paris: Vrin.

Ferraris, Maurizio. 2001. *Il mondo esterno*. Milan: Bompiani.

————. 2014. *Manifesto of New Realism*. Translated by Sarah De Sanctis. Albany: SUNY Press.

Frege, Gottlob. 1974. *The Foundations of Arithmetic*. 2nd ed. Translated by J. L. Austin. New York: Harper & Brothers.

Gabriel, Markus, ed. 2014. *Der Neue Realismus*. Berlin: Suhrkamp.

————. 2015a. *Why the World Does Not Exist*. Malden: Polity.

————. 2015b. *Fields of Sense. A New Realist Ontology*. Edinburgh: Edinburgh University Press.

Gettier, Edmund L. 1963. "Is Justified True Belief Knowledge?" *Analysis* 23 (6): pp. 121–123.

Girard, Jean-Yves. 2006. *Le Point Aveugle: Vol. 1 Cours de Logique. Vers la Perfection*. Paris: Hermann.

González, Juan C. 2004. "El argumento de la alucinación revisitado." *Acta Comportamentalia* 12 (3): pp. 55–73.

Husserl, Edmund. 1979. *Aufsätze und Rezensionen*. Edited by Bernhard Rang, Husserliana XXII. Den Haag: Martinus Nijhoff.

————. 1994. *Early Writings in the Philosophy of Logic and Mathematics*. Translated by Dallas Willard. Dordrecht: Kluwer Academic Publishers.

Kölbel, Max. 2008. "Introduction: Motivations for Relativism." In *Relative Truth*, edited by Manuel García-Carpintero and Max Kölbel, pp. 1–38. Oxford: Oxford University Press.

Lindgaard, Jakob. 2008. *Experience, Norm, and Nature*. Oxford: Blackwell.

Malcolm, Norman. 1952. "Knowledge and Belief." *Mind* 61 (242): pp. 178–189.

Martin, Michael G. F. 2004. "The Limits of Self-Awareness." *Philosophical Studies* 120 (1–3): pp. 37–89.

McDowell, John. 1984. "De Re senses." *Philosophical Quarterly* 34 (136): pp. 283–294.

————. 1994. *Mind and World*. Cambridge, MA: Harvard University Press.

————. 2008: "Reply to Travis." In *Experience, Norm, and Nature*, edited by Jakob Lindgaard, pp. 258–267. Oxford: Blackwell.

————. 2009. *The Engaged Intellect: Philosophical Essays*. Cambridge, MA: Harvard University Press.

Meillassoux, Quentin. 2010. *After Finitude. An Essay on the Necessity of Contingency*. Translated by Ray Brassier. London: Bloomsbury Academic.

Merleau-Ponty, Maurice. 1958. *Phenomenology of Perception*. Translated by Colin Smith. London: Routledge & Kegan Paul.

Plato. 1953. *The Dialogues of Plato*. Translated into English by Benjamin Jowett. Oxford: Clarendon Press.

Putnam, Hilary. 2005. *Ethics Without Ontology*. Cambridge, MA: Harvard University Press.

Recanati, François. 2004. *Literal Meaning*. Cambridge: Cambridge University Press.

————. 2007. *Perspectival Thought: A Plea for (Moderate) Relativism*. Oxford: Oxford University Press.

Richard, Mark. 2004. "Contextualism and Relativism." *Philosophical Studies: An International Journal for Philosophy in the Analytic Tradition* 119 (1/2): pp. 215–242.

Shakespeare, William. 1899. *The Tragedy of Hamlet*. Edited By Edward Dowden. London: Methuen.

Soteriou, Matthew. 2009. "The Disjunctive Theory of Perception." *The Stanford Encyclopedia of Philosophy (Summer 2020 Edition)*, edited by Edward N. Zalta. https://plato.stanford.edu/archives/sum2020/entries/perception-disjunctive/.

Stojanovic, Isidora. 2008. "The Scope and the Subtleties of the Contextualism / Literalism / Relativism Debate." *Language and Linguistics Compass* 2 (6): pp. 1171–1188.

Strawson, Peter. 1966. *The Bounds of Sense*. London: Methuen.

Travis, Charles. 2000. *Unshadowed Thought: Representation in Thought and Language*. Cambridge, MA: Harvard University Press.

———. 2004. "The Silence of the Senses." *Mind* 113 (449): pp. 57–94.

———. 2006. *Thought's Footing*. Oxford: Oxford University Press.

Waismann, Friedrich. (1936) 1996. *Einführung in das mathematische Denken*. Reprint, Darmstadt: Wissenschaftliche Buchgesellschaft.

Wittgenstein, Ludwig. 1974. *Philosophical Grammar*. Edited by Rush Rhees. Translated by Anthony Kenny. Blackwell: Oxford.

Index of Names

Index of Subjects